Hertfordshire
COUNTY COUNCIL
Community Information

− 1 OCT 2001

10/4

Lilley

Years

uiling

ease renew/return this item by the last date shown.

that your telephone call is charged at local rate,
ease call the numbers as set out below:

	From Area codes 01923 or 0208:	From the rest of Herts:
enewals:	01923 471373	01438 737373
quiries:	01923 471333	01438 737333
nicom:	01923 471599	01438 737599

2

es

D1513164

Dedication

This book is dedicated to countless customers, members of the staff at
W. Eaden Lilley & Co Ltd, present and past, and all those associated with
the company throughout its 250 years history.

Hertfordshire Libraries, Arts and Information	
H40 481	1526
BC	10\00
	£12.00

© Eaden Lilley, 2000

Published by W. Eaden Lilley & Co. Ltd,
Market Place, Saffron Walden, Essex, CB10 1HR, United Kingdom.

All rights reserved. No part of this publication may be reproduced, stored in any retrieval system or transmitted in any form or by any means, electronic, mechanical, photocopying, recording or otherwise, without prior written permission of the copyright holder for which application should be addressed to the publishers. No liability shall be attached to the author, the copyright holder or the publishers for loss or damage of any nature suffered as a result of reliance on the reproduction of any of the contents of this publication or any errors or omissions in its contents.

ISBN 0-9538400-0-X

Designed, printed and bound by

TSG Creative Solutions, 105 Great North Road, Eaton Socon,
St. Neots, Cambridgeshire, PE19 8EL, United Kingdom.

Authors Note

No book of this type could have been written without the help and support of a great number of people, who happily gave of their time as the story of this fascinating company unfolded.

I am particularly grateful to those who invited me into their homes, and then quietly told me of their work and involvement with W. Eaden Lilley & Co. Ltd, in many cases a lifetime's connection.

All the senior executives at the store, particularly Eaden Lilley and Michael Marriott, have supported and encouraged the book, and have helped me discover old documents, photographs and pieces of history.

Much research, especially of the very early days, was carried out by Dennis Heath, and a host of other people have helped including Bob Francis, Sara Coveley, Carole Ormes and Mitzi Holmes.

The staff of The Cambridge Collection and the Cambridgeshire Record Offices have, as usual, gone out of their way to help provide information. Colin Grant, editor of the Cambridge Evening News speedily granted permission for several extracts from their newspaper to be used.

The following have allowed me to quote from their books:-

Phillimore & Co Ltd for Victorian Cambridge: Josiah Carter's Diaries, by Enid Porter; Edward Arnold for British Economic and Social History, 1700-1982, by C.P.Hill; Penguin Books for The Buildings of England, Cambridgeshire, by Nikolaus Pevsner; Cambridge University Press for Annals of Cambridge, and The Cambridge Social History of Britain, 1750 - 1950, Vol.2, and Salamander Books for Victorian and Edwardian Cambridge .

12   W. EADEN LILLEY & C° LIMI

SHOW ROOM

Contents

Author's note

Chapter One

History in the making   *1 - 7*

Smart boys wanted   *8 - 9*

Chapter Two

Love and scandal   *11 - 19*

The customer's last contact   *20 - 21*

Chapter Three

Drink and a bubbling business   *23 - 30*

First impressions   *32 - 33*

Chapter Four

Growth in the Victorian age   *35 - 42*

Value for money   *44 - 45*

Chapter Five

High standards and high quality   *47 - 53*

A job for life   *54 - 55*

Chapter Six

A task of "extraordinary interest"   *57 - 64*

A hard act to follow   *66 - 67*

Chapter Seven

No news is good news   *69 - 78*

A family affair   *80 - 81*

Chapter Eight

Are You Being Served?   *83 - 90*

Mr Kirkup's happy kindergarten   *92 - 93*

Chapter Nine

"Energy, willingness, interest, ability"   *95 - 101*

Blue serge to grey flannel   *102 - 103*

Linking the generations   *104 - 105*

Chapter Ten

The fateful decision   *107 - 120*

12   W EADEN LILLEY & Cᵒ LIMITED

Chapter 1

History in the making

John Purchas pulled his short waistcoat over his rounded stomach and a little closer to his black breeches, adjusted his white stockings, and prepared to take his daily constitutional around the streets of Cambridge. He donned his dark blue frock coat and picked out his gold headed cane before heading out of the property in Shoemaker Row and setting off smartly towards Market Hill.

He had some 40 minutes to spend before his meeting and he had worked out a route that could be taken at a reasonable stroll and would still allow him time to take another look at The Globe public house in Bridge Street.

The 45-year-old shopkeeper was in a fine mood, the May sunshine reflecting his comfort in life. He smiled at those he met, he moved back to allow a lady to pass, he praised the weather and chatted briefly to acquaintances in the streets of the city. The day was, in a small but important way, a milestone in the life of the man whose perspicacity and skill were starting to reap the rewards that he sought and deserved.

Checking his fob watch he paused outside The Globe. It required some money spent on it, but it seemed a reasonable investment. He would think about its potential.

Now he strolled back towards his business, its sign creaking gently in the breeze. The printer was already in the shop, and both men stood closer to the open wooden shutters better to inspect the copper printing block that had been produced. Some billheads had been prepared, and they held them up to the light so that the shopkeeper could read: "Bought of John Purchas. Haberdasher and Mercer in Shoemaker Row. The top right of the bill declared: "Cambridge 17 ," the actual date to be written by hand against each sale.

The warm promise of that day in 1750 had been richly rewarded. John Purchas and his wife Martha were delighted with the new billheads, and later, as the business expanded, were to add in a different type "Oil-Man" meaning someone who sold coloured oils and paints.

The John Purchas billhead of 1750

More than 200 years later a billhead from the business was found. That happy discovery added to the archives of one of the country's most illustrious department stores which has been a backbone of life in the City of Cambridge through trials, tribulations, wars, joy and heartbreak. The eventual closure of Eaden Lilley in June, 1999, brought sorrow and tears not only for its workforce and management, but to those who regarded it as a stable part of their lives, used by generations of the same families.

The closure of the store, just six months before its 250th anniversary, provides a final chapter, but its sparkling and fascinating history contributes a wealth of stories as we dip into its past.

The year 1750 does offer a convenient start to this story and for many years the Eaden Lilley sign outside its store proudly proclaimed "Established in 1750." We can, however, go back a lot further in establishing the links of business and site, but perhaps we should start in 1676 when John Purchas rented the premises from Richard Pearson, a cordwainer (shoemaker). John's son Joseph married Richard's daughter Anne, and in 1712, describing himself as a "mercer and merchant tailor" took over the business from his father, and the property in Shoemaker Row from his father in law, paying £100 for the lease plus a "peppercorn rent." Two years later he bought the premises. He and Anne had one son, John, and three daughters Ann, Elizabeth and Mary. Joseph died in 1721 - the same year that Walpole became England's first prime minister - and in his will left the business and a house in Green Street to his widow for her lifetime. John was only 16, but it was clearly expected that he would take over the business when he was older. To each of his daughters Joseph left the then considerable sum of £500.

Eleven years later, when John was 27, his mother transferred her life interest in the business and property to him "for and in recognition of the mutual love and affection which she hath and bears unto her son and toward his preferrment and advantage in the world."

The handover may well have been encouraged by the marriage of John to Martha Jardine, the daughter of a Scottish woollen merchant, who, with his brother, had settled in Cambridge and like so many of his contemporaries attended the independent chapel in Downing Place. There is a strong possibility that the Jardine brothers were used as a model for the brothers in Charles Dickens' Our Mutual Friend.

The story of religious dissenters is one that will figure during some of the history of Eaden Lilley, and from time to time has an influence on affairs. The famous Cambridge Intelligencer newspaper was, in the late 1700s edited by Benjamin Flower the son of a prominent dissenter, and was to develop new reporting skills and comment that was to be cursed by the government of the day. On the whole the established church appeared to rub along with the dissenters, but every now and again there was an outbreak of unrest or violence, sometimes involving smashing the offices of the newspaper. Usually, however, matters were kept well in hand. Richard Jones, for instance, who in 1750 was minister of the Green Street Presbyterian Church in Cambridge, featured in The Gentleman's Magazine, which said: "Without betraying his principles, he lived in harmony with all members of the University, and with many of them in the strictest intimacy and friendship."

Dissenting ministers were not allowed to solemnise marriages, with the result that John and Martha were married at the chapel of Katharine Hall - now St Catherine's College.

White thread, blue tape and "Dutch Prettys" are included in this bill of sale presented to Isaac Aspland for items "bought of John Purchas" in April 1750

The Cambridge that John Purchas knew so well had plenty of charm, a wealth of logistic problems and a certain reluctance to keep up with the great events that were taking place in the country. The chief market place was Market Hill, a few steps away from his shop. Here, on Saturdays, it was particularly well stocked with butter made up into pounds and half pounds, each being a yard long for the convenience of the college butlers cutting into what they called "sizes." In his book Annals of Cambridge (1) C.H.Cooper says the city also had a butchers market, a herb market and a fish market. He says that fuel was tolerably reasonable, considering Cambridge is an inland town 50 miles from the sea, and that wine was brought up from Lynn by water and sold wholesale or retail from taverns licensed by the University. Water craft were unloaded at Great Bridge Quay, and there were 11 letter carriers licensed by the University; five went to London, one to Bury St Edmunds, one to Downham Market, one to Lynn, one to Northampton and one to Norwich. There were two stage coaches to London.

The roads of Britain under George 11 were in a pretty bad way; dustbowls in the summer, quagmires in the winter, although the Turnpike Act was starting to have some effect in Cambridgeshire, Huntingdonshire and Hertfordshire. It allowed tolls on road users with the money being earmarked for the repair and maintenance of sections of the roads. By 1750 there were about 400 Turnpike Trusts, although mainly over small sections of roadway. They too, caused problems, with road users unenthusiastic about paying the tolls; riots flared up from time to time, but long term the tolls had a marked improvement on the roads.

Shopping in Cambridge had its difficulties, particularly in bad weather when the unpaved roads were deep in mud and rubbish thrown out from shops and houses. The shop signs were large and dangerous as they projected into the street and reportedly caused some fatal accidents. By 1760 it was forbidden to have signs overhanging streets.

Shoemaker's Row boasted several shops including a baker, a brazier and an ironmonger. The business of John Purchas certainly had haberdashery, linen, drapery and mercery, and later included all oils, pitch, tar, rosins, alum, soap and vinegar. Paints were made on the premises over the next 200 years, usually under the "Cambro" brand name.

The historic university town had about 10,000 inhabitants, but that figure was dramatically increased in August and September when the annual Stourbridge Fair was held on land near the Newmarket Road still known as Stourbridge Common. Writing in the East Anglian Magazine (2) Bron Surrey explained: "Working busily, the vendors, from rich merchants to cheap-jacks who had flocked to Cambridge from all parts of England and even Europe, transformed the area into the likeness of a small town. Shops were arranged in rows like streets, each trade having its own row and each row its corresponding name - Haberdashers' Row, Booksellers' Row, Cooks' Row, Garlic Row, Cheapside and many others. In the centre of these streets was a great square, called the Duddery from the woollen clothes or 'duds' that were sold there, with enough space for waggons to drive into it and load and unload at the doors of the booths.

"Meanwhile the town itself and all the villages for miles around had begun to fill with 'prodigious crouds' of visitors, and lodgings were at such a premium that the 'very barns and stables are turned into inns and made fit as they can to lodge the meaner sort of people.'

"Fifty hackney coaches plied night and morning to and from London, and enterprising watermen went so far as to bring down their Thames wherries by road on waggons in order to hire them on the Cam like buses between the centre of Cambridge and the Fair."

If these were heady times for the Purchas family and the good citizens of Cambridge they were doubly so for the people of Britain who were living under the authority of George 11, described by one publication as "self-important, methodical, fussy, hard-working, petty-minded, and a skirt-chasing little man.

"He presided, without great enthusiasm, over a period of unprecedented prosperity for Britain at home and abroad. It was the heyday of the English aristocracy, whose great and beautiful houses studded the land."

In one of the regular disagreements with the French, George became the last reigning King of England to lead troops into battle which he did at Dettingen in 1743, when he defeated the old enemy.

These were also the days of famous and infamous activity. April 16, 1746 saw the bloody battle of Culloden where the English led by the Duke of Cumberland made short work of the Jacobites of Bonnie Prince Charlie. The slaughter that followed earned the duke the title of "Butcher Cumberland."

The very stuff of history was being carved out in Britain and abroad with names like Clive of India, William Pitt and later General Wolfe.

How much of this touched the working men and women of Cambridge is hard to judge, although the city was quick to celebrate victories whenever they were recorded.

John Purchas continued with the task of running his business, which, according to his contemporaries, earned him the reputation of being parsimonious.

For the financially astute man there was another benefit when his mother died in 1752 and left him her copyhold in the manors of Witchford and Wentworth on the Isle of Ely and Cambridgeshire, and a residual interest in her estate in Chesterton.

His passing interest in The Globe public house developed into a major expansion when he bought the property together with five other public houses in the city - The Castle in Castle Hill, The Three Hawks in Sidney College, The Compasses at Peterhouse, The Boot in Green Street and The White Horse in Castle Street.

Now here was an important and influential man, and he became active in civic affairs, not least of which must have been the problems being faced by the city over high wheat prices, with disturbances reported from many parts of the United Kingdom. In June, 1757 a mob, "chiefly of women, assembled at Cambridge and broke open a store house in which lodged about 15 quarters of wheat, the property of a farmer who that day refused an offer of 9s 6d a bushel for it, and carried all off." (3) The same happened the following day when the mob "having intelligence of 27 sacks of flour, and despite the effort of local constables, they broke open the store and made off with it."

Two years later he gave two silver stoups - quart sized mugs - to the corporation which bear the Purchas arms on one side and the corporation arms on the other, and a year later he was appointed Mayor of Cambridge. The silver is on show today in the City Council Chamber.

The Reverend William Cole described Purchas as "eminent" and said he was a "professed Presbyterian or Independent," yet despite that "luckily by some manner or other he was a supporter of the official corporation candidates for parliamentary honours."

Alderman John Purchas, who started our history, died in 1764, aged 59, and was interred in the family vault at Holy Trinity Church. In his will he made provision for the loyal Martha, left £20 to his servant Joseph Ansell and left the remainder to his son John, then aged 26.

He followed his father's skill in managing to walk the same tight rope between religious and civil affairs, and also became Mayor of Cambridge, the first time in 1771, the same year that he joined the so-called "Great Meeting" in Hog Hill, a Presbyterian church which had been legally established in 1687 by the Declaration of Indulgence. In 1696 the "Great Meeting" accepted Congregationalism, and those who objected joined Green Street Presbyterian Church.

John was five times mayor of the city.

He also became a brewer, having been left a share in a brewhouse in Mill Lane. Later he acquired. The Angel in Allwins Lane. He was described as an "eminent common brewer of St Clement's."

In the country, now under the mentally disturbed King George III, things were not going well. The American Declaration of Independence of July 4, 1776 had outraged the King, some of his parliament and many of his people. British forces had defeats inflicted on them by the Americans under George Washington and offers of assistance against the British flooded in from Spain, France and The Netherlands. The eventual loss of the colonies, and recognition of the United States of America, was a mighty blow for many.

Cambridge, like other cities, used the few victories for celebration, including a great fireworks display in June 1780 on news of the surrender of Charlestown.

Whether because of ill-health or because of the demands of his brewing interests John Purchas decided to dispose of the business in Shoemaker Row and in 1782 sold to Joseph Hart, "his trade and stock in trade consisting of a variety of articles in the said trade and the lease of the house and premises." Hart then formed a partnership with Joseph Ansell, who had been an apprentice of the old John Purchas.

The sale included various materials, silk stuffs, crepe, masquerade, Venetian silk cord, Durant (glazed woollen material), black nesella, taminy, tammy, oils and colours.

The partnership agreement is interesting and throws some light on the nature and conduct of the business, according to research by Dennis Heath now in the Eaden Lilley archives.

Ansell and Hart were to be partners "in the business of haberdashery and other branches of haberdashery, linen, drapery and mercery, together with all oils, pitch, tar and other articles sold by John Purchas".

The business was known, unsurprisingly as "Ansell & Hart, successors to Mr Purchas," and carried out in the premises in Shoemaker Row. As Hart was to live in the house he had, according to the partnership agreement, to "provide a proper person to light the Counting House fire" - the only room to be heated in winter - and keep the Counting House, warehouse staircases and passages, clean. The premises were to be jointly owned and all rates, rents and repairs to be paid for out of joint stock and profits, as were all assistants and apprentices. All married assistants were to be paid weekly, and single men to be boarded and lodged in Hart's house for which he would receive a "reasonable recompense." No women assistants were to be employed.

The partners engaged to "diligently employ themselves about the business of the joint trade, to be true and just to each other in all dealings." There was provision for annual accounts, a division of dividends and what action should be taken in the event of the death of either partner.

Joseph Ansell's stock of knitting worsted, cutlery ware and other articles was not to be brought into the joint business, but along with millinery, lace and gauze would continue to be sold in his own shop by his wife and daughter, who could also serve at the partnership shop.

The inventory of stock taken in December, 1784 and running to 50 pages, was valued at £4060 8s 11d. The inventory of fixtures and fittings valued at £142 1s 9d, gives an idea of the shop premises and living accommodation. The Counting House, clearly considered the most important room, contained a double desk with draws and cupboards, mahogany bookcase, other bookcases, a stove with Dutch tiles and cheeks, a map of England, money scales, a candlestick, two extinguishers, three inkstands and more.

From the same inventory we discover the shop had three counters, two pairs of brass scales with their boxes and 10 small weightstands to weigh a total of just under 14lbs. There were also copper scales, needle boxes, more inkstands and a bell with a pull from the Counting House and street door.

The property also consisted of several small warehouses, a garrett containing among other items a bedstead with a yellow woolsey covers and a quilt, a middle garrett and a back garrett, a kitchen, a pitch warehouse and an oil warehouse, largely used for the manufacture of paints. Some of the equipment was still in use 100 years later when George Heath started in the oilshop. His enterprise was to expand the operation into the hardware and grocery departments that grew from the end of the 19th century.

Having settled his business affairs John Purchas made his will in February, 1787 and died a month later leaving his estate, including his brewing interests to his eldest son, but providing for his second son William Jardine Purchas to receive £5000 on reaching 21.

And so the business progressed for another six years until Thomas Hovell replaced Joseph Ansell in 1788 and it became known as Hart and Hovell. Not too much is known of Thomas Hovell although he was a Mayor of the city, and landowner. He voted in the 1802 elections where his poll register was recorded as "gentleman", and his signature is among those of the trustees of the Hauxton to Dunsbridge Turnpike Road. He owned property in Trinity Street and built a house on the Leys Estate.

The archives of Eaden Lilley hold a small but fascinating receipt for carriage for Hart and Hovell for a cask of snuff delivered to Dr Thomas Pinkerton of Paisley to the value of £1.7.10d.

By 1793 the business was firmly in the hands of Thomas Hovell & Company, and by 1798 two new names appear alongside that of Hovell. One is P.K.Staples and the other is William Eaden, who had married Elizabeth Hart, the daughter of Joseph Hart one of the partners who had taken over the business from John Purchas in 1782.

This is the first mention of an ancestor of the company. The son of William Eaden and Susannah York, the aspiring youngster was shortly to become a sole partner and later a sole owner of the business that was to flourish into the family owned department store that was known and admired by so many.

The 19th century held the promise of adventure, wealth and excitement for the 27-year-old in the business of Hovell, Staples and Eaden.

(1) Annals of Cambridge, by C.H.Cooper, Cambridge University Press, 1908.

(2) East Anglian Magazine, Volume 5, September, 1964.

(3) Cambridge Newspapers and Opinion, 1780-1850, by Michael J. Murphy, The Oleander Press of Cambridge, 1977

Smart boys wanted

L anding a job at the "Store of Repute" in the early 1900s was the dream of many a youngster fresh from school.

They were tough times around and during the First World War, and any income that could be added to the often meagre family finances was more than welcome.

"Smart boy wanted" signs in the windows of Eaden Lilley invariably encouraged a substantial interest, and one of those pleased to capture the job of van-boy was 15-year-old Reg Constable who started at "Lilleys" on April 1, 1917. His task was to hold the head of the van horses while they were being loaded and unloaded, and help deliver goods.

A similar task fell, in 1921, to the 14-year-old George Pope, whose driver was a Mr Thurlow with the mate of Gus Reynolds.

"The horses were very well cared for and had to be groomed, harness cleaned and brasses shining every day" he recalled many years later*. "They were stabled at Mill Lane, which was also used as a warehouse for furniture and bedding."

It was the role of van boys throughout time to put up with some tough moments, and the young Pope, standing with his horse outside the store in the pouring rain had made the mistake of sheltering from the downpour under the horse's head, where he was discovered by director Walter Lilley. He received no sympathy for his plight but instead was on the sharp end of the director's tongue for not making sure the horse was properly protected from the weather.

The horses rejoiced in the names of Prince, Jimmy, Rosie, Arthur, Beauty and others, and were given a day off a week from their not too difficult duties.

Food also figured large in the life of the van boy and the annual garden party given by Mrs Walter Lilley at her home in West Road was a golden moment. For helping to clear up afterwards teenager Pope and colleagues were given ice-cream and bags of buns left over from the feast.

It didn't always, however, work out as expected. Delivering some furniture to a property in Mount Pleasant the van boy was delighted to see the lady of the house come outside with a large piece of cake. As he licked his lips in anticipation he was horrified to see the glorious confection fed to the horse.

Disenchanted with his lot as a van boy young Pope found himself in the office of his manager, a Mr Winterbottom, asking for a better position.

"He asked what I wanted to do. I hadn't thought of that, but I quickly replied 'Upholstery, Sir' because I remember having seen an advertisement somewhere.

Later he became an apprentice for three years at the princely sum of just under 2p per hour - and he had to buy his own tools and apron. The workshop was in Sydney Street and later in Mill Lane.

Reg Constable "moved inside" after a year on the vans, and helped in the packing room of the drapery department.

The horses rejoiced in the names of Prince, Jimmy, Rosie, Arthur and Beauty

The threat of Zeppelin raids during the war years provoked a fear largely out of proportion to the limited damage the airships could inflict, but nonetheless the thought of being bombed from the sky was frightening to many people. Eaden Lilley made an effort to ease the pain by an early warning system that was simple and presumably fairly effective.

On hearing that a raid might be on its way an employee was detailed to go to the front of the premises and ring a handbell. He also rang the bell when it was "all clear." Passersby were, presumably, able to distinguish between the two bells!

Another "smart boy" to take up a job at Eaden Lilley between the wars was D.A.Murfet, who joined in May, 1936, having answered an advertisement for the toy department. His working hours were 8.00am to 6.00pm during the week and until 7.00pm on Saturdays, with a half day on Thursdays. His wages, 10s per week.

His day started with sweeping the floors, dusting and removing the wrappers over the goods. At 8.30am the senior staff arrived and the others went to breakfast in the canteen under its manager Miss Penny. They were back at work by 9.00am.

The toy department was in the Martin Hall throughout the year but expanded to the whole of the second floor from November to Christmas, where it was called TOYLAND.

"On my first Christmas Eve I was allowed to go home early, at 9.00pm, while the others stayed to 10.00pm," he remembered.

Later he took a three year apprenticeship with the furnishing department which was cut short by his war service with the Royal Air Force. He returned in 1946 and was made a buyer in 1958 and then buyer of carpet and lino departments in 1964.

Contracts over the years included carpeting Masters' Lodges at the University, work in other colleges and stately homes, and the carpets in the Trinity College rooms when Prince Charles was in residence.

"Smart girls" were also required. Miss Juffs started work in 1919, aged 14, in the corsetry and babywear department. Her wage was 5s a week.

"We were dusting from morning to night, and we had to save every piece of string we could because it was in such short supply," she said.

All parcels had to be taken down a cobblestone yard at the side of the building for packing and then delivery by handcart, later by horse drawn carts.

Every morning the formidable Mr Gates stood by the entrance to check timekeeping of the staff.

Miss Juffs also helped with window dressing and was a relief for the switchboard, which had three extensions.

* Over the years Eaden Lilley has asked retiring employees to write down some of their memories of their time at the store, and the above recollections are taken from those notes.

Chapter 2

Love and scandal

I t was, of course, a scandal and the glorious talk of society in the city and the county.

The thought that the beautiful young Eaden girl should have run off with a man nearly 20 years her senior, was the delicious conversation of the ladies over their tea cups, and the men over their beer.

The families themselves were distraught. William and Elizabeth Eaden could not believe that one of their four daughters should have taken such action. To elope with a farmer's son and then wed at London's Marylebone Church was almost beyond belief.

But the young Elizabeth had scampered off with David Lilley, one of nine children of Bourn farmer Edward Lilley and his wife Sarah, and the deed was done. The family would have to accept the inevitable.

And like all scandals it was edged into the background by other events, many from outside the country. The good citizens of Cambridge and those around Great Britain had been deeply shocked by the French Revolution, which was welcomed by radicals and dissenters, but deplored by Royalists and Loyalists. Church and King mobs made life difficult for the radicals, and the dissenters often found themselves on the wrong end of Loyalist fury.

An extremely uneasy peace between Britain and France, which had been roughly pulled together in 1802, fell apart a year later, and the country found itself at war again, this time against the increasing might of the forces organised by a young Corsican officer, Napoleon Bonaparte who declared himself head of the French government and then in 1804 assumed the title of emperor.

George 111, who was suffering from bouts of mental and physical illness, was obliged to recall William Pitt to the post of Prime Minister, a position he had quit after the King refused to allow any gesture towards Catholic emancipation.

The death of Nelson at the Battle of Trafalgar in 1805 plunged the country into depression. His death, said The Times, was "too great a price for the capture and destruction of 20 sail of French and Spanish men of war."

Three years later William Eaden found himself one of two sole partners of the shop in Shoemaker Row, which, by now, was flourishing, despite some opposition being shown to trade in the city. A letter to the Cambridge Chronicle complained that "the characteristic of Cambridge is the seat of Learning, not of Trade."

In 1816 a bonny boy was born to the former runaways, and perhaps in deference to the previous problems, was named William Eaden Lilley. His early life, education and training pointed him in the direction of the family business, and there is no doubt that as a youngster he must have spent some considerable time running through the Shoemaker Row shop, helping with the chores and becoming thoroughly acquainted with the business.

Market Street, c.1870s, with Holy Trinity Church on the left, and the Macintosh's first shop.
When the firm moved to the opposite side of the road the site was used for the Henry Martyn Hall.

His grandfather clearly showed an active interest in young William, and there are references in some of his personal notebooks to amounts spent on the youngster. When the boy was 17, for instance, grandfather paid a total of £13.2.0 to send William and his mother on a trip to London.

By 1833 William Eaden had become the sole owner of the Cambridge shop, with stock valued at £11,300, a considerable amount in those days. His personal cash book throws some light on aspects of life in a country now ruled by the "Sailor King" William IV.

The housekeeping for Mrs Elizabeth Eaden was mostly £2 a week, but from time to time was increased to £5 a week. Her daughter was given an allowance of £2 a week.

Food prices were detailed as three fowls, 5/6; 21 1lb rounds of beef, 10/-; turkey at 7/-; shoulder of lamb, 2/11; goose, 6/-; calves head, 3/-; four gallons of raspberries, 9/-; three dozen apricots, 7/6; six pigeons, 2/-.

Hair cutting and corn cutting both cost 1/-.

William Eaden seems to have been fairly eclectic in his religious donations, which include 11/- to the Irish Baptist Mission, 5/- to the Clothing Society, £1 to the British and Foreign Bible Society, £2.2.0 to the local hospital, £1 to the Wesleyan Meeting and £1 for the erection of chapels in Jamaica.

His former partner Thomas Hovell, was the recipient of a barrel of oysters at Christmas,1834 and another barrel in 1835.

Although the population of Cambridge was still quite small by modern standards many people lived in the centre of town, and houses backed so close to Great St Mary's Church that those going to church could clearly see into the bedrooms. In front of these and across a narrow street stood a square of more houses and shops. According to A.Gray in his book The Town of Cambridge, a History" (1) the market square itself was little more than a very broad street which started generally in line with Rose Crescent. The market cross stood not in Market Hill, but at the end of a broadened out Petty Cury.

The infrastructure was, however, improving in other ways. In 1823 the streets were first lit by oil-gas and soon afterwards John Grafton, who had started a business in London, opened a gas retort in Gas Lane, Barnwell, and contracted with the city commissioners to light the streets with "inflammable air or gas obtained from coal." In 1834 a company was started to take over the business.

Cambridge itself was also at some pains to keep the "new fangled" railway system away from its colleges - as was Oxford - but although it was the subject of fierce debate, verbal and physical, the steam driven locomotive was making its mark, and it is estimated that between 1830 and 1850 the rail system was effectively laid down across the country. The railway actually came to Cambridge in 1842. The Eastern Counties Railway Company gained parliamentary approval to construct a railway from a junction at Newport in Essex, through Cambridge to Brandon. The University's stiff opposition resulted in the two potential town sites for a station being rejected, and eventually it was built a mile away "in a most inconvenient place in green and largely swampy fields."

In 1837 William Eaden died, and for a short while his wife Elizabeth ran the shop, which was pretty much the same in size and style as in the days of John Purchas. A stock book, dated 1839, which is held in the Eaden Lilley archives, lists a variety of items, including grey calico, 27in wide, which sold at 4d a yard; single size Witney blankets at 4s4d a pair; coloured gingham at 6d a yard and women's worsted hose at 11d a pair.

These were, however, difficult times for trade. Chartism which called for political reform and trade unionism among other things, was at its height, there was a general depression and business was poor, not least in Cambridge, with its relatively small population of about 24,500.

The stock book was produced in the same year that 23-year-old William Eaden Lilley took over the business, and the same year that he married Katherine Smith. His training at the hands of his grandparents appears to have been a success, and he was trading as draper, carpet warehouseman, paper merchant, and a seller of oils, colours and brushes.

The young man's move into ownership of the shop coincided with one of the most remarkable periods in Britain's history. Queen Victoria was crowned at Westminster in 1837 and, although there were still plenty of problems, the country was heading into a period of sustained prosperity and growth. The wars against France had effectively ended with the Battle of Waterloo in June, 1815; the problems of the post-war years had subsided; the industrial revolution was providing employment and investment for many - although job losses for others - the repeal of the Corn Laws was providing better times for agriculture, and by the 1840s it was beginning to be a good time for the country, and a goodly number of its citizens. Education was taking on a brighter stance and the barriers against dissenters being allowed into university were being lifted.

All of this, of course, sounds good in the round, but on an individual basis life was as complicated as ever, particularly if, as a teenager, you had to deal with the vagaries of a housekeeper like Mrs Goody.

That was the unfortunate lot of 15-year-old Josiah Chater who came from Saffron Walden in Essex to work at "Eaden Lilleys Drapery Shop" where he was to be trained in book-keeping and to help in the shop.

Working conditions for shop assistants anywhere in Britain were tough, with long hours and poor pay, although most had food and accommodation provided. Even as late as 1883 a 16 hour working day was quite common for assistants in shops throughout the country.

When Chater joined the employees at Eaden Lilley he was lodged in Market Street next to the shop - the name of the street had by then been changed from Shoemaker Row - and came under the dreadful gaze of Mrs Goody, whose husband also worked in the shop.

She was a tough and demanding lady who kept a close eye on her charges, and was heartily disliked by all.

During his time with the shop Josiah's hours varied according to the time of the year and the workload; for much of the time a 9.00pm closure was normal, but after a while the shop closed at 7.00pm in the winter and 9.00pm in the summer.

It was common for the apprentices to sweep out the shop and "counting house" before breakfast, working by candlelight in the winter.

Josiah had the good sense to keep a diary which faithfully recorded his days, and "The Chater Diaries" have been carefully edited by Enid Porter in her book, Victorian Cambridge (2) .

Clearly the hours worked and the amount of food consumed played a vital role in the youngster's lifestyle, and there are plenty of references to both.

> *"We got up at 7 o'clock this morning. Stephen and I dressed ourselves and at 8 o'clock a large bell was rung and in to breakfast we went in good earnest. There was a round of bread and butter cut for each and laid on a plate, and the rest of the loaf was on the table so that the rest we cut ourselves.*

> *"We had boiled leg of mutton and dumplings for dinner - the bell was rung again at 1 o'clock. We also tea'd exactly at half past four. After I left the shop I went into the house for supper - had cold mutton and cheese - and after supper Cook and I had a game of chess.........We have a new looking glass in our room, also night candlesticks and all the necessary requisites."*

At other times of the year excessively long hours were demanded. Stocktaking was one.

On January 27, 1845, dealing with listing the stock, he wrote:

> "Stephen and Cook got up this morning at a quarter past three to take down the haberdashery. When I came down they were making some toast and chocolate for breakfast, so I got a slice of plum pudding and a sausage roll and so made a very good breakfast. After breakfast Mr Best and I did the carpet warehouse and we finished that completely this evening, and Mr Blumson and Stephen have nearly finished the warehouse upstairs."

And two days later:

> "Mr Lilley came down before breakfast and 'checked over' the landing and Barrett's place......this evening they began on the shop. John and I took down the haberdashery on his side excepting the ribbons; Mr Lilley 'called over' the greater part of the drapery side. We did not go into supper till half past ten."

He described stocktaking as "that most odious of all work" which was a "little hindered" during the day by the customers.

The end of stocktaking, however, brought a chance to celebrate, and once again the details were faithfully recorded by Josiah. On February 20, 1845, he wrote:-

> "At half past seven we met at the Coach and Horses in the Cury and had a good supper of sausages, hot potatoes, and bread and beer - we could not eat them all so I pocketed two sausages, and two large pieces of bread for lunch tomorrow, Mr Blumson took four, Hayes three and the rest some each, so that we cleared the dishes. After supper we had pipes and ale, and some had brandy and water and cigars, and we broke up just at ten o'clock......Mr Blumson treated me. Some of the sausages were brought home for Stephen as he could not come; Mr Hayes is now warming them at the fire in the counting house, on the cinder shifter with a piece of board laid on it, so it is quite clean."

The fairs held in Cambridge were also demanding for the workers and management at Eaden Lilley. On September 25, 1846 Josiah spent a little time in his room completing the diary, and was able to write:-

> "We have had an extraordinary day of business, both in saddlers and other wholesale customers. Have not been so busy for a long time, and being one porter short we have had as much as we could fairly manage...........It has been a very good fair, but goods were dear."

And a year later:

> "This is Horse Fair Day and we began early to be busy, and busy we were all day long. I did not leave the counting house till ten o'clock, which is late now as I generally leave on Saturdays by nine. It has been the fairest fair we have had since I have been here."

Records of employment kept by the company show that Josiah was earning £10 a year in 1847, which was increased to £15 a year in 1848, which was paid in two tranches, one in August and one in March. The following year two payments made a total annual salary of £20, and by 1850 it had increased to £25, which seems to have been on a par with other draper's shops.

Discipline was strict, the finer points of procedures and tribunals were not around to worry employers. Josiah recalled:-

"The first thing this morning Sheldrick took six shillings for a stone of soap, but only put 3/6d in the till, keeping 2/6d for himself. He was detected by Reece, but he stoutly denied it and said he must have dropped the money. But Reece saw him put his hand in his pocket as he stooped down to look for it, and he saw the 2/6d in his hand and told him so. Sheldrick denied it, but would not show his hand, and afterwards the 2/6d was found against the rag basket, four yards from the place where he took the money. So when Mr Lilley came down he was acquainted with the circumstances. He had a policeman in and Sheldrick was taken to the Town Hall, examined and remanded till tomorrow. Reece had some suspicion of him last Saturday and had told Mr Lilley."

After work the diarist appears to have taken life at a gallop with walks to Coton and Grantchester, a visit to a circus, skating, the University May races and more.

"Mr Lilley went over to Waterbeach this afternoon which gave me an opportunity of getting away a little earlier in the evening, so that I got to Mr Smart's very little after eight. They were then playing at charades, so I joined them and capital fun we had. Then we went to supper and after that we had a game at Twilight; I had three forfeits and we had rare kissing. After that we had Cross Questions and Crooked Answers - we broke up a little after eleven. There were about 24 there altogether, 12 young ladies and 12 young gentlemen. I certainly had not spent such a merry evening for many a day. Just as I was coming away I could not find my hat, so I went home in a bargeman's worsted cap with a long red and green tassel to it."

Josiah was also involved in what he called "gypsy parties", and which we now call picnics. He was invited to one in June, 1848:

"Of course I worked well this morning and when Mr Lilley came down I asked for the afternoon which was readily granted. At three o'clock I went over for my charges, Agnes Barrett and Susannah Macintosh, but they were gone on, so I cut after them and caught them at the Mill Road railway gate. We had a hot and long walk, but afterwards came the treat, for at tea we all sat on the grass. After tea came cricketing and sundry other games, and a delightful walk to the chalk pits where are the best scenes across Cambridge that I know of. We came back and set the ladies all racing, and at nine we all cleared up and departed. It was a most splendid day. The walk home I enjoyed most, as we were occupied in conversation on very rational and intellectual topics which we (my two ladies and I) discussed with spirit. There were about 16 or 18 of us in all, a nice round party, and very agreeable indeed."

It is interesting to note that the names mentioned by Josiah were names associated with other businesses in the city centre, Smart's the tailors, Barrett's china and glass merchants and Macintosh's hardware merchants.

The diaries also give us a glimpse of William Eaden Lilley, a man in his 30s, during the time of Chater's employment.

In June, 1848 Josiah recalled that his employer was concerned about how the apprentice was spending his leisure time.

"Soon after Mr Lilley came down this morning he called me in and asked me why I and Cook wished to go out together, and I told him where we were going. Then he began a short harangue saying I might perhaps think him inquisitive in wishing to know, but he only intended it for my good. He said it was not well for me to associate too familiarly with the ladies so as to give them an opportunity to think that I meant more than I intended. But what he said, and the sentiments he expressed were administered with such a kind spirit that I could not take it otherwise than an act of kindness on his part......he said he liked me to have pleasure and would always do so when opportunity afforded, and therefore Cook and I might go...........

Costumes, mantles and laces were all available at W.Eaden Lilley & Co., store at 12, Market Street pictured at the turn of the century, although the basic layout and look of the store is likely to have been very similar in previous years.

And in case you worried about whatever happened to the tiresome Mrs Goody you may be pleased to know that she was dismissed in 1846, and she, Mr Goody and her family left Cambridge. She was replaced by a Miss Aitkin, and Josiah confided to his diary that "I do not dislike the look of her at all."

She was clearly the bearer of good tidings because she provided "some very good bread and cheese and we are having a washing stand and its accompaniment".

Later Chater left the firm to set up his own fabric, and then accounting firm. He married Agnes Barrett, and they had 13 children.

Although Eaden Lilley's shop could not at this stage be called a department store, the idea of different departments in one shop was starting to take off, and in 1852 in Paris the famous Bon Marche department store was opened offering a woman "everything she needed under one roof." Similar moves were taking place in Britain with Bainbridge's in Newcastle, Caley's in Windsor and later William Whiteley's in Bayswater. The expansion of Eaden Lilley's into a department store was to take place later, largely after it became a limited company in 1890.

And so in the mid-Victorian period of stability William Eaden Lilley - who had married a second time to Rachel Martha Palmer - settled into developing the shop and its business, although there must have been a period of extreme concern in 1849 when a great fire consumed parts of the city, destroying eight houses and damaging many more. Ten fire engines attended and everyone turned out to help fight the fire with "chains" of men passing buckets of water from the river in Garret Hostel Lane.

The habit of haggling over shop prices was more or less over by the 1840s. A Frenchman visiting this country in 1850 reported that if an attempt was made to negotiate a lower price the "shop assistant thinks at first that you have misunderstood him, but when he understands what you are driving at, he stiffens visibly like a man of honour to whom one has made a shady proposal."

The Cambridge shop owner, in line with others throughout the country, also had to deal with the vexed question of credit. Many shops simply refused to give credit; others, like Eaden Lilley, had a more subtle approach to the problem. A magnificent little book, discreetly labelled "Reference Book" appears in the archives of Eaden Lilley, and clearly deals with the problem of credit by the use of references. Applications for credit were obviously considered, and approved or rejected according to the references that could be made available.

The first noted in the book - although there were probably earlier versions that have not stood the test of time - shows as July 24, 1858 and deals with Captain J.W.E.Smith of Grantchester who is described as a "Staff Officer of Pensioners."

The keeper of the book records that Captain Smith stated that he "possessed landed property and was known to Mr Easter, who called and said he knew his family and that of his wife to be of high respectability."

On March 1, 1860 Edward Maris, a draper, made another appeal for credit after it had previously been declined. He told the recorder that he had "just taken stock" which was valued at £300 and that he had "good book debts of £400, and an estate which cost £400 and could now sell for £500." He apparently had debts to "secondary parties" of £300 and "to Fosters for £100 for which his father-in-law was answerable."

The clue to success or failure of the applicants appears to lay in a red inked tick next to each name. Mr Maris was awarded a tick.

A goodly number of the applicants were drapers who clearly bought their products through Eaden Lilley on a wholesale basis.

In April, 1860, J.Richardson a draper of Haverhill, applied having taken over "the business of Pearce, who when he called said that Richardson had property of his own to an amount of £200 to £300."

There was, however, a little concern over Miss M. Robinson of Little Downham, a former "housekeeper at Elbornes's." Her references were passed direct to William Eaden Lilley who "only knew generally that she was respectable and had an unsettled claim against her late masters."

The phrase "credit control" which almost certainly had not been heard of in Queen Victoria's time, obviously applied to the family business of Eaden Lilley, even in the 1800s. Several references in the little metal clasped book refer to limiting the credit to a fixed amount, perhaps £30 or £50, and sometimes to a fixed reference. Walter Fordham of Bourne, for instance, had monies of his own, and his reference was a Mr Payne. The recorder of the book insisted that he be informed should any other security be proposed.

Land, property or good references appeared to be the key to success. Thomas Browning of Kingston, for instance, was introduced by Miss Banks. They were about to be married and wished to open an account. A Mr Garner P Luny offered a reference, which was enough to earn the celebrated red tick.

Thomas Goodwin of Bassingbourn, was granted credit to a "moderate amount" after his reference wrote that he was a man "of good business habits and ability. I think he will make his way. I believe his means to be about £300, and he has borrowed some capital on Easy Terms."

With sadler J.Gross of Hopton the store was told by his referee that he "was quite safe for the amount you name" - £10 to £30.

The credit facilities, so carefully organised and arranged, were helping to strengthen the operations of the drapery, floor coverings, soft furnishings and oil shop in Market Street. Now a dedicated staff, nearly all men, lived, worked and breathed Eaden Lilley, while the owner bustled around his empire. The comfortable economic times helped the business and expansion was all around. William himself, now the father of 11 children, was a determined dissenter, and was involved in a variety of city projects. And, in the years ahead, he was to turn his attention to that most awful of subjects, the "evil of drink."

(1) *The Town of Cambridge, a History, by A. Gray, published by Heffer.*

(2) *Victorian Cambridge, Josiah Chater's Diaries, by Enid Porter, published in 1975 by Phillimore & Co Ltd., Shopwyke Manor Barn, Chichester, West Sussex.*

Memories

The customer's last contact

Driving through the crowded streets of London and out towards the docks was a difficult journey at any time, but in May, 1926 it became particularly hazardous.

Railway and bus stations, the docks, other strategic points and many street corners were guarded by armed troops and a host of special constables. Armoured cars escorted supplies as they were ferried through the city, and thousands of angry workers lined the roads chanting "Not a penny off the pay, not a second off the day."

For this was the General Strike called by the TUC in support of the miners strike, and its supporters included dockers, transport workers, printers and builders.

The government, being better organised than the TUC, had set up a series of emergency measures, and trains, lorries, buses and trams were driven by volunteers, often middle-aged men and undergraduates. The result was a bubbling cauldron of dissent with outbreaks of violence and the windows of trams and other vehicles smashed by the workers.

A fine selection of the Eaden Lilley vans and vehicles in the 1920s and 1930s

Into this chaos, confusion and danger came the little vans of Eaden Lilley's store in Cambridge, their drivers charged with the task of fetching goods from the docks which could not be delivered by any other means. Somehow they dodged the worst of the troubles, and there are no records of how many journeys were made during the nine day strike.

As an indication of the risks being run it is worth noting that more than 3000 people were arrested for being involved with acts of violence during the short strike, which resulted in a complete victory for Baldwin's government. A year later it made general strikes illegal.

One of the drivers involved in the dock runs was Arthur Bunting who had joined the firm in 1922 when horse drawn vehicles were still being used for deliveries aided by a few motor vans. Within a few years the horses had gone and 12 smart motor vans carried out the delivery tasks on town and country runs within a 30 miles radius of Cambridge. The vans were also used to provide chairs, tables and other items used when the company provided the catering at various functions.

Between 1924-25 the company garage was opened in Glisson Road, and the larger premises "enabled the garage staff to carry out our own maintenance and repairs" recalled Arthur Bunting many years later.

During the Second World War six of the Eaden Lilley vans were commandeered for the war effort and petrol rationing reduced the deliveries that could be made by the remaining vans.

The role of the transport delivery service and the vanmen's duties were detailed in anonymous documents in the company archives. It recorded that on "town delivery days" it was usual to use certain vans for the parcels service and others to deliver furniture. On "country days" it was normal for all vans to carry general goods unless a complete load of furniture could be made up to warrant a special van.

At least one vehicle had to be held back every day for special deliveries, which included transfer of stock from the warehouse to the store. "The main reason for this," said the scribe, "is to promote more selling space in the store."

Special deliveries also included a sudden request for food or goods, and an example was given in the documents of a customer who urgently needed some sausages for her lodger's evening meal. They were rushed by van to her house, and the cost involved was justified by the company writer who explained; "In the general running of a good store it is these little things, customers seemingly petty requests fulfilled, that often bring big business. The customer is looking for service and satisfaction from all departments."

And the work of the vanmen themselves was also emphasised with the point that "they are often the last members of the staff in contact with the customer. It is often the case that good business can be lost by the unwillingness of delivery men to fulfil some small request by perhaps some lady living alone who wants an item of furniture moved from one room to another, or who wants something returned to the store that is either faulty or sent in error. Or perhaps a can or bottle to refill.

"A vanman needs to be a pleasant helpful type of person, for whom nothing is too much trouble."

The vanman's other duties included looking after his vehicle, which included regular checking of tyre pressures, engine oil, distilled water in the battery and other items. It was also his duty to keep the van clean as "a well looked after van is one of the best forms of advertisement for the firm, especially if groceries and provisions are sold."

It was common practice for a driver always to keep the same van, and in some cases a bonus was given at the end of each month for safe driving and cleanliness.

The driver was also responsible for his load although in some cases there was a "Statutory Attendant" - better known as "a mate."

In the early days it was standard practice for companies to buy the vehicle chassis and then have the body built according to requirements.

Later, costs of coach built bodies meant that the system was changed to complete vans that only had to be painted in the Eaden Lilley livery.

SHOW ROOM

12   W. EADEN LILLEY & C⁰ LIMI

Chapter 3

Drink and a bubbling business

By the bright clear light of an oil-lamp 60-year-old William Eaden Lilley bent over the table and carefully wrote down his thoughts and plans for the formation of a new society in Cambridge.

Working quickly in his private accommodation at the shop in Market Street he produced a series of notes, and prepared his speech for the inaugural meeting of the Cambridge Total Abstinence Union. As a town councillor, a businessman, a father and a dissenter, he had some fairly unequivocal views on the "evil of drink" and he intended to make those views crystal clear to those who attended the meeting.

His private papers, held in the Eaden Lilley archives, include the notes he prepared for the speech on that night in 1877. They include sections that have been underlined, some crossing-out and inserts marked Cx and Dx, which were intended to be included in other parts of the speech. They were all neatly written in brown ink on cream paper.

His speech intended to hail those men, who years before, had encouraged and practised the habit of teetotalism.

"Many of these men I knew, for let me tell you they were not likely to let any one known to sympathise with them, be ignorant of their existence, or of the institutions whose cause they advocated with such lively and persistent enthusiasm."

And warming to his theme he wrote: "I am here tonight to record with feelings of deepest gratitude the self-denying laborious persistent efforts with which these men followed and persuaded their erring and fallen fellow men, not always indeed with success, but sometimes achieving glorious good in snatching from utter ruin the souls and bodies of those who had become slaves to drink."

He expected there to be plenty of examples presented during the evening showing the "evils which now result from the present force of drinking habit among our people." He would content himself with the recent comments of a judge, as an example "which is entirely sufficient for my purposes."

The unnamed judge said "that but for drink we might shut up nine-tenths of our goals.

"As to the existence of this need in our own town, I feel confident that the personal experience of everyone present is likely to be able fully to confirm it, my own memory goes back to cases which illustrate this need among the rich and poor, the highly educated, the tradesmen, the very ignorant, the young and the old."

The Union was officially formed at that meeting in 1877, and according to the records the organisation "devoted its energies to uniting men and women in temperance work without regard to creed or party." The first officers were president, William Eaden Lilley; vice presidents the Rev. A.E.Humphreys and the Rev J.Martin plus three more, and there was also a treasurer and secretary. It had a separate women's committee.

The CTAU held public meetings, circulated literature and provided speakers for other organisations until 1880 when it ceased to exist.

The first William Eaden Lilley who presided over the company during the Victorian years of prosperity.

These were the years of mid-Victorian prosperity and drive, although thousands of workers living in squalid conditions and under regular threat of dismissal may not have agreed with the overall view. Much of the wealth and stability of the nation was built by people like William Eaden Lilley who carefully developed their business, made enough to live a pleasant lifestyle and were constantly aware of the need to reinvest in the business. In later years, towards the end of the 19th century, we will see how the shop expanded and how the directors took advantage of the Limited Liability Act of 1855 to reduce the risk of bankruptcy.

Towns like Cambridge were still small by today's standards, with a population in 1841 of about 24,500.

In his book Victorian and Edwardian Cambridge from old photographs (1) author F.A.Reeve explains that travellers were arriving in the town by coach even after the introduction of the railway in 1845, and that the stage coach ran between Cambridge and Bedford until 1894.

"Huge eight-horse waggons transported goods, and herds of oxon and sheep passed through the town on their way to market or to London.

"The river trade was still important. Horses towed strings of barges, some with masts and sails, as far as Midsummer Common, then the bargees used stout poles called 'spreads' along the backs of the Colleges."

Even the university was small. In 1849 there were 1,775 under-graduates, and only 355 matriculated in 1851. The borough was jointly administered, says F.A.Reeve, by the Town Council and the Improvement Commissioners, the "latter being responsible for paving, drainage, lighting, sewage disposal, plans for new buildings and infectious diseases, but in 1889 the number of councillors was increased, university representatives were included, and the Board of the Improvement Commissioners was abolished."

From the 1870s onwards the number of bicycles increased dramatically, amazing visitors to Cambridge

At the shop, as far as we can tell, business bubbled along successfully, and there are still accounts and other financial documents around to support the theory. The firm did, however, have its problems. The low lying fen country continued to hurl floods and unexpected torrential rain at the town and its inhabitants. In June, 1858 the shop operating from 12, Market Street advertised a "reduced prices" sale of "wetted drapery and carpet stock" which consisted of about 2,300 yards of Brussels and tapestry carpets, and about 1,200 yards of hemp, Union Kidderminster and Dutch carpets.

The damage caused "during the late storm" also affected "printed druggets, mattings and mats, rough brown, Hollands, Scotch sheetings, linen, ticks and beddings, grey and white calicoes, table clothing, sheetings, canvasses, blankets, flannels, ironing cloths, table baizes, women's brown cotton hose, knitting worsted, strings" and a lot more.

Business and his life as a dissenter sometimes presented problems for the shop owner. There seems at this time to have been little love lost between the dissenters, who were mostly the tradesmen in the town, and the church. In 1861 the Rev. G. Williams, vicar of Hauxton asked William Eaden Lilley for a donation towards the £420 required for the repair of the church nave and tower. As a dissenter the shop owner felt that his convictions would not allow him to make a voluntary contribution to the church, and much discussion, and later letters, followed, concluding with a rather pompous note from the vicar who said: "It is for you to decide whether or not your connexion is likely to be increased in a business point of view by its being generally known that you hold such extreme views."

Unable to take such a challenge without response the shop owner sent two letters to the vicar, and in one he wrote: -

"Dear Sir (then the 'dear' was crossed out)

"When you called I told you truthfully the state of my mind, and I have at times thought of it since, notwithstanding a considerable pressure of business, and my inclination was to have left you £5. Your letter has now settled this question, and I am unable to give you a donation and preserve my self-respect."

Two years later he was on the list of trustees for the building of Barnwell Workmans Hall, where the problem of the demon drink again reared its ugly head. The appeal leaflet explained:-

"The ill-fame of Barnwell is, we fear, familiar to all, and much better known than the strong religious movement which for many months has been going on in the place. Every Sunday five or six hundred working men, the largest part of whom are from the most careless and practically godless class, crowd to hear a simple exposition of the Gospel and many of these are now reclaimed drunkards, and devout God-fearing men.

"It is now felt that some further step must be taken to counteract the attraction of public houses, as well as to provide those who have withdrawn themselves from their debasing influences, with some place where they can procure the means of self improvement and healthy recreation."

The problem that was causing such aggravation to the dissenters and others was the opening of public houses on a Sunday which was introduced by the Sale of Intoxicating Liquors Act in the mid 1850s. It was to be a running sore for churchmen and the temperance movement for many years. Among the documents in the private papers of William Eaden Lilley is a "flyer" headed "Should the Sale of Intoxicating Liquors on Sundays be discontinued?" Unsurprisingly it came up with a great number of words showing that "about three million" UK residents were anxious to see an end to Sunday drinking.

The mid 1850s saw Britain involved in more than its fair share of wars including the Crimean War which resulted in the deaths of 4,600 British lives plus 13,000 wounded and up to 17,000 who died of disease; the war in Persia and the Indian Mutiny of 1857-58.

At home Lord Palmerston formed his second administration in 1859 with Gladstone as Chancellor of the Exchequer and Earl Russell as Foreign Secretary. There were some dramatic times in the 1860s, many of which would have affected the little community at Cambridge including widespread bank failures during the 1867 financial crisis in England.

In the town itself Mathesons' directory of 1867 showed William Eaden Lilley's shop at 12, Market Street explaining that it was a "draper, linen, carpet and warehouseman, wholesale paper merchant, oil, colour and brush warehouse." Its merchandise had changed little in 100 years.

The storms that had caused such damage to Eaden Lilley's stock in 1858 returned with a vengeance in the August of 1879 when the rivers in Cambridge rose by eight feet and for two days complete havoc was caused throughout the region. Eaden Lilley's and Robert Sayle's shops recorded damage of up to £2,000 each.

By 1883 William Eaden Lilley, who was by then 67 and a widower, decided to hand over the reins of power to his 42-year-old son, also William Eaden Lilley who, a year later, went into partnership with Stephen Mansfield, described as a "warehouseman" of Cambridge. Their business was to be warehousemen, drapers, hosiers, stationers and general dealers.

The carefully preserved agreement between the two men shows that the joint venture should be carried out under the name of William Eaden Lilley and Company, with the capital of just under £28,000 provided by William Eaden Lilley. The bankers were to be Messrs Mortlock and Company of Cambridge, and there were strict arrangements about the sums of money to be taken out of the business by the two men.

A whole series of restrictions bound the partners together, not least that they should not "take any apprentice or hire or dismiss any clerk, traveller, workman or servant" without the consent of the other partner.

William Eaden Lilley was the senior partner with a two-thirds holding and entitlement to profits while Stephen Mansfield retained the other third.

The agreement was signed by both men in the presence of James Spearing, a solicitor of Cambridge.

From this point onwards matters started to be put on a more formal basis at the Market Street shop, and by January 1888 the partners had decided that the business should be controlled by a board "with the view of securing more leisure for ourselves." The board was to consist of chairman William Eaden Lilley, vice-chairman Stephen Mansfield, secretary F.D.Prior and the other directors being Philip Lilley, Alfred C.Mansfield and Edward Moore. The board was to meet every Monday morning, with the "opening of letters" at 8.50am by the chairman and vice chairman, with "special care being taken not to open any letters that may bear evidence of a private nature."

Other letters affecting the business, including complaints from customers, were to be discussed by the board.

The same arrangements applied to telegrams, which were still fairly new in the towns outside London. The telegraph was first used in Britain in 1837 and taken over by the Post Office in 1868 - cable links to the United States and India were established by 1870. The telegraphic address for Eaden Lilley & Co was "Lilley, Cambridge."

Details of holidays for board members - three weeks per year to be taken in two parts if at all possible - dinner and tea arrangements, security and other matters were initially arranged.

The company warehouse in Market Street in 1886

The board also agreed to a one year trial of a bonus system for directors and employees. A total of £700 was to be provided for distribution during the year ending December, 1888; two-thirds to go to Philip Lilley, Alfred Mansfield and F.D.Prior and the rest to be divided among salesmen in the drapery, carpet and wholesale department and the oil shop, and the clerks in the Counting House.

The first real board meeting was held on January 16, 1888 when the new arrangements were confirmed and explained to the employees. Staff bonuses ranged from £1 to £12.

For the employees, however, there was a snag. In a move that would have been appreciated by the chairman's father - who had died in 1884 - the newly formed board decided that the sum formerly allowed for beer money was to be discontinued, and the ordinary bonus of the year would be increased by the same amount.

The day-to-day and week-to-week operations of the company were carefully reported in the board minutes. Appointments and changes in staff were added on a regular basis, journeys for board members approved, decisions on whether to buy or sell horses confirmed and financial details debated and discussed. They also looked at physical expansion for the company and applications for planning permission were duly lodged with the Borough of Cambridge authorities. On August 9, 1888 the council approved an Eaden Lilley application "for permission to construct areas under Market Street in front of premises there, under their own occupation." Interestingly the conditions that applied have not changed much in more than 100 years; the fee to the council, however, has changed. In 1888 there was an annual payment required by the council for the extra construction of two shillings.

Property extensions by the store really started in 1888 with the acquisition of 23, Market Street. In the years ahead many more extensions were to claim buildings in Market Street, Market Passage, Sidney Street and Green Street.

At the same time the number of employees increased; the company now boasted about 40 staff apart from the board members working in seven different departments. Salaries ranged from up to £600 per annum for senior directors, £300 for the company secretary and down to £25 or less for salesmen.

Reorganisation, a clearly defined strategy and steady economic conditions helped in the development of the company which for the first half year of 1888 saw sales reach £42,585, an increase of £2,786 on the same period of the previous year.

The sales were later to be helped in part by a deal agreed with Liberty & Co of London. The Cambridge store agreed an agency operation and opened a separate Liberty department in September, 1888. The goods were sold at Liberty prices and included art fabrics and specialities. It was a bold step for Eaden Lilley and required stock purchase of "at least £200." The London store provided circulars, books of patterns and designs plus 50 per cent towards a £20 advertising campaign.

The shop at 12, Market Street was being "refixtured" in the autumn of 1888, and departments were being moved to 23, Market Street. The company marked the changes with a sale of stock that might have been soiled in the improvements. They included dress materials, mantles, jackets, calicos, linens, flannels, tablecloths and napkins, lace curtains, fancy muslins, umbrellas, hosiery and gloves, haberdashery and other items. At the same time in the new premises they were offering "past season's stock of Brussels tapestry and velvet curtains, tapestry curtains, linoleum and more at a great reduction."

The board heard that the "Great Clearance Sale" held on September 8, 10 and 11, 1888 had resulted in "very satisfactory results."

To stay within Government restrictions the top floor of the new building had been carefully measured and showed 6,880 cu feet which would allow for the accommodation of 27 workgirls.

The company was also looking at training its staff and several workers were involved in different schemes. Miss Bilton and Miss Kirkup, for instance, were sent to lessons at the "Scientific Dresscutting Association." The result, a few months later, was that the dressmaking department was enlarged with ladies' fitting rooms provided on the first floor. Special attention was to be given to mourning orders which were to be undertaken at the "shortest notice."

Some 5,000 copies of a circular apologising to Eaden Lilley customers for the inconvenience during the store's alteration were distributed. It concluded: "We shall endeavour in every way to merit the continuance of that good opinion and favour which has been accorded to the firm and its predecessors now through so long a period."

During the remainder of the year the board dealt with a variety of matters including deciding to appeal against the borough council assessment of £225 for 23, Market Street. It was later reduced to £200. They also agreed to distribute meat and poultry as Christmas gifts to the married male employees.

As they headed towards their Christmas break the partners and directors of the company could add a spring to their step safe in the knowledge that they had progressed the business, and the more adventurous could look to the immediate future which promised even more good news.

The following year saw a welter of moves by the company, a new lease for property behind 23, Market Street; extra accommodation for salesmen who lived "above the shop"; more staff for the dress department; the lease of stables in Petty Cury; remodelling of the warehouse including the development of an iron bridge between properties; the possibility of using gas to power the lift in the store, and some firm instructions for employees over Christmas, who were not allowed to leave "by an earlier train than is necessary for them to reach their destination".

The "New Unionism" which was being established through much of the country following the strike of the women match workers of Bryant and May in London, appears to have passed by W.Eaden Lilley & Co., or if it was there the strength of support was not enough to trouble the board members and senior management.

By 1890 events were conspiring to support some major developments at the Cambridge store. Stephen Mansfield was taken ill, and the partnership was terminated on January 27 of that year. The chairman moved swiftly to form the firm into a limited liability company, a move met with "cordial acceptance" by the board members. As we have seen the Limited Liability Act of 1855 limited responsibility of investors in the event of bankruptcy of the company. This Act eventually encouraged the vast growth of business throughout the country.

The new company was duly registered, and its capital was detailed as being £75,000 divided into 5000 preference shares of £10 each and 2500 ordinary shares of £10 each. The premises were 12, Market Street which was held on lease "from the Chancellor, Masters and Scholars of the University of Cambridge" for a term which expired in December, 1916 at an annual rent of £130, and 23, Market Street which was held on leases from the Corporation of Cambridge for 75 years from March 1888 at a total annual rent of £100. The freehold house and premises of 35, Bridge Street were also included in the new company's assets. The change over netted William Eaden Lilley, "the vendor" some £72,000 which was allotted in £47,200 worth of preference shares and £24,800 worth of ordinary shares which was issued to "the vendor or his nominees." The properties were also bought by the company for just under £50,000.

In the same month the board placed just under £300 for distribution among the staff as a bonus for the past year. The amounts ranged from £1 to £14. A staff supper was organised for the last day of that month, and on February 1 an interesting notice was issued to employees which revealed that in future the amount available for bonuses would be doubled. The deal was couched in such a way that employees could look forward to substantial returns if they pulled their weight. Nowadays the notice would, no doubt, be attacked as being patronising and offensive but in the second month of 1890 it must have provided blissful reading for those employees who had been with the company for more than two years.

The bonus distribution, said the notice, was "subject to the proviso that every servant included in the arrangement has performed his work and conducted himself in a manner entirely satisfactory to the Directors.

"In making the distribution the Directors will carefully consider the circumstances of each individual and will endeavour to do exactly right to each one according to their best judgement."

The offer was described as being "purely voluntary" by the board with the absolute right to decide any question that may arise over the distribution.

"The effect of this determination to augment the bonus, should be to create, by the common effort in view of the division of profit, and with the energy that this provokes, an increased return, sufficient to fully justify the step which has been announced and which should enrich the staff and not impoverish the Directors.

"It should ever be remembered that one has not only his own interest but those of his fellow-assistants in his keeping.

"It will be evident that if all, as one man, be banded together to give fair trial to this experiment, and promote the success of the Company, that very gratifying financial results will follow, while in the conduct of the business, much friction will be avoided, greater correctness secured and a healthier tone be observable all round."

New staff were regularly taken on at W.Eaden Lilley & Co. Ltd including in March 1890, F.E.Welford, who was taken on trial for a salary of £20 a year. Years later he was to set up his own cannery business in Norway and used to call on George Heath at Eaden Lilley to sell his products under the Welford label.

Figures produced in the first quarter of 1890 show that the largest department at the store in terms of turnover was the wholesale department, followed by the drapery, carpets and others. Last of all was the oil shop.

Changes, modifications and developments were all around, presumably at a pace to encourage Fred Martin to boldly ask for an increase in wages as he was planning to get married. He, like all other sales assistants at the time, had signed the Assistants' Engagement Book which was held by the company.

It required the incoming employee to "agree to serve to the best of my abilities as packer in consideration of your paying me a salary at and after the rate of eight shillings per week, and to abide by all rules and regulations now in force, or that may be made for the management of your establishment and that one day's notice shall be sufficient to terminate this agreement."

The final 10 words were to haunt the youngster. The board decided at its meeting on July 29, 1890 that they "could not offer sufficient to justify his marrying and resolved to request him to find other employment."They relented a little later by allowing him to continue in service until he found another job - provided he did not get married.

Domestic arrangements for the staff were shifted to Bridge Street; more stables were leased and those in Petty Cury rented out, and a night watchman was employed to patrol both Market Street premises. The company's period of major expansion was now close to hand.

---

(1) *Victorian and Edwardian Cambridge from old photographs, by F.A.Reeve, published by Batsford, 1971.*

W EADEN LILLEY & C° LIMITED

Reputable but old fashioned is a complaint that has been made against Eaden Lilley from time to time - and not always from customers.

When George Wells arrived to start work at the store in September, 1926 he was less than impressed with what he saw, and nearly turned round and went home again.

The old fashioned image of the store changed in 1928 when several departments at 12, Market Street were upgraded, including the millinery section

Number 23, Market Street provided " an old fashioned shop front", and inside he found "two long counters, with four disused elaborate gas brackets hanging over one. These supported a double row of brass case tubing the length of the counter, which was used to display antimacassars, cushion covers, mantle borders and other items. Most of these goods my previous shop did not even bother to stock."

But his first impressions were soon changed. Despite its antiquated looks the store did a brisk trade, and George Wells was soon plunged into the October rush. In those days students and their parents used to order curtains and loose covers for their college rooms, due to be fitted by the first Tuesday in October. It meant a great deal of extra effort for the girls in the workroom.

For Jean Butler who started at the store a year earlier her immediate impression was of the shopwalkers, Arthur Rutt and C.Aves. "They met potential customers at the door, inquiring which department they required, and escorted them to the counter before pulling out a chair and making sure there was an assistant to serve them," she said later.

Apprentice S.Williams who joined Eaden Lilley is October, 1930 was not wildly impressed with a starting wage of 7/6d a week plus meals - which rose to 15/0d per week after four years - but he was mightily struck by the wonderful breakfasts served by Mrs Shadbolt at 8.30am every day. He spent the first year in the dress materials department, then the Manchester department, and then mens department.

In the early days he started work at 8.00am and had to take the wrappers off the counters, dust the chairs and carefully place them in front of the counters ready for customers. Each night the rolls of material had to be freshly turned to stop the material from creasing. He also had to make up the pattern books with small pieces of material for customers to inspect.

From time to time Walter Eaden Lilley would arrive in the materials department and ask young Williams to measure three yards of material, not to be cut but marked with a pin. Later he would come back and check the measurements were correct. "Often he said the measurement was a few inches too much," remembers the former apprentice who eventually worked for the firm for 21 years.

The first meeting that George Wells had with Walter Eaden Lilley was two months after he had started work when he was asked how he was settling in and whether he was comfortable in his lodgings.

"I explained that my lodgings at 22, Maids Causeway were comfortable, but I was looking for others as I was charged 30/- a week and the more usual rate was 21/-. He appeared very sympathetic, and I wonder now if the managing director of any other firm would have taken that much interest in the problems of a junior assistant."

The three former employees all had a host of other memories of the 1920s and 30s including the shock of discovering that the normally solemn Armistice Day commemorations each year, were turned into a Rag Day in Cambridge "with decorated floats and undergraduates in fancy dress penetrating the workrooms, kitchens and rest rooms at the firm."

And mannequin parades held on the fashion floor in the spring and autumn, with gold painted chairs for the customers..

And customers in the linen department who wanted to know the warp and weft of sheets and the count, 60 to 80 on some, 100-100 on very fine cotton.

Bunting for the decorations at May Balls was made up in the workroom, together with many other special jobs, recalls Mrs Daynes who worked in that department, but absolute priority was given to hospital orders. Scissors were supplied by the firm. Staff had to provide their own needles and thimbles - and pay for the scissors to be sharpened.

There are memories too from customers who used the shop at that time. Schoolboy Colin Henderson took his mother to the shop in 1936, shortly after she had recovered from an operation, to buy her a birthday present. Together they decided on a wicker needlework box, costing 3/6d. It was bought in the department under Henry Martyn Hall, and was used by his mother until her death, then by his wife where it was in regular use until she died in 1997, and remained in "excellent condition."

And he has fine memories of Christmas at Eaden Lilley as a boy, where he could visit Father Christmas. "A switchback railway, which ran along a good length of one of the upper floors, was used for the journey to the grotto," he says.

Superb boxed French railway sets were on sale at £8, too much for the Henderson family, although Christmas morning nearly always included a new signal box or gantry; one year a magnificent box of lead soldiers.

SHOW ROOM

12 W EADEN LILLEY & C° LIMI

Chapter 4

Growth in the Victorian age

The January night was bitter cold as the watchman tramped round the warehouse in Cambridge checking to see that all was well and the property was secure.

The glare from his lantern illuminated barrels, packages, cloth and stock for the shops of Eaden Lilley, a firm called Stockbridge and A.Mackintosh & Son.

Suddenly something caught his eye and he held the lantern high to catch the movement. Within a second the flame of the "safety lantern" ran up the funnel, licked across his fingers and burnt deep into his flesh. With a mighty curse he dropped the lantern which immediately burst at his feet and to his horror ignited oil which had leaked from barrels nearby.

In moments the premises in Market Passage were burning fiercely and shouts rang out for water and the fire brigade. Members of the Conservative Club, which backed on to the warehouse, rushed out and together with a group of undergraduates set to providing chains of water in the battle against the flames. The fire brigade arrived and pumped water on to the blaze which by now had engulfed much of the property.

To add to the confusion a rumour quickly spread through the gathering crowd that gunpowder was stored on the premises and fearful residents set to dragging their furniture and other property from their homes.

It was several hours before the blaze was brought under control, the residents took their furniture back in, and some semblance of normality returned to the little community. Initial estimates of damage were put as high as £6,000, which in 1892 was a great deal of money. That, presumably, included the cost of the building which was destroyed. The damage to Eaden Lilley's stock was confirmed at £400, with the other two shops suffering similar losses.

A claim by Eaden Lilley, which was only insured for £250, was lodged with the Norwich Union, and paid in full.

The fire coincided with a flurry of activity around the end of 1891 and start of 1892 which included correspondence with the Early Closing Association where the store agreed to close the premises at 7.00pm during July, August and September, providing "the majority of our trade does the same."

The Thursday afternoon early closing, which was to become such a feature of life in shops and stores, was also agreed for the months of January, February and March. The moves were, no doubt, encouraged by various Acts of Parliament which were passed to regulate and reduce the long hours of shop assistants; the one in 1892 confirmed that the maximum hours to be worked by assistants under the age of 18 were not to exceed 74 a week. Ten years earlier the Shop-Assistants Twelve Hours' Labour League had been formed, but it had been a tough battle to reduce the working hours to anywhere near that level, and by the mid 1880s the Early Closing Association reluctantly confirmed that only a small minority of London stores accepted the half day closing.

January 1892 also brought more good news for the staff, now numbering about 60, when a hand-written letter from chairman W. Eaden Lilley was circulated. It confirmed that the financial results for the previous year had shown a "considerable increase" over the previous year, and that extra premises had been secured.

Despite the extra cost of the new building - at 24 Market Street - the board had decided to increase the annual bonus which they hoped "would stimulate the staff to renewed efforts in the future."

There was, however, a little sting in the tail with a note that "much valuable time is being taken in the rectification of errors," according to the Counting House, and that "some might have been avoided with ordinary care and attention."

In a surprisingly enlightened comment for the period the circular said that the board would gladly welcome any suggestions by their employees for the benefit of the business.

The millinery and dressmaking departments at Eaden Lilley at the end of the 19th century were looking to the styles of the "New Woman" that had been encouraged in the call for female emancipation. Emily Pankhurst, leader of the British suffragettes had formed the Women's Franchise League in 1889, but it was to be a few years before the more militant approach was to secure the vote for women.

Nonetheless fashions, as always, were changing, although at the end of the century waists were still tight and skirts were long. The craze for bicycling did mean that clothes were less hampering, and a new freer style was developed for other sports including tennis.

Long trailing skirts were on their way out, although leg-of-mutton sleeves remained according to the fashion requirements of the day. Corsets stayed as women of all ages struggled to meet the 18in waist laid down as the ideal size.

Men only days out for Eaden Lilley staff in 1882 for a trip down the river....

....and to a theatre in 1901 with the Second William Eaden Lilley, front row centre.

The woman's place was still in the home or at least in the store as far as the directors were concerned. In May, 1892 they agreed to organise a day's outing at the seaside for all employees - as long as they were men ! The trip, to Hunstanton in Norfolk, included lunch at the Sandringham Hotel. It cost a total of £29.12s, plus £1 for tips.

Cambridge still had a relatively small population of less than 40,000, and in the 1890s there were still no streets or houses beyond the Hills Road railway bridge.

But it was not free of traffic, horsedrawn or bicycle, and services were operated by The Cambridge Street Tramways Company, together with hansom cabs and growlers. And there will always be accidents. In April,1892, an Eaden Lilley employee, detailed as B. Kidd, had the hard luck to be hit by a cycle ridden by a Salvation Army official. He was off work for two weeks.

For the store to work properly it needed horse-drawn vans and wagons. It also needed stables, and several moves were made to acquire better or bigger stabling in the town centre. The buying and selling of horses, started on an ad-hoc basis a few years earlier, began to take on a more important role, and by the early 1900s the operations consumed a lot of time and effort, as we shall discover in the pages ahead.

The work of American Thomas Edison and Englishman Joseph Swan in developing the incandescent electric lamp in the 1870s had not been fully grasped by many towns in Britain. Gas lighting worked and was cheap and there seemed little point in changing. It was not until August,1892, for instance, that Eaden Lilley looked seriously at the possibilities of using electric light for their premises at 12 and 23, Market Street and the New Warehouse in Market Passage, which was still years ahead of many stores and shops, and it was only by the early 1900s that many new houses could boast electric power points.

The early and mid 1890s saw expansion of premises and staff at Eaden Lilley with the 1893 acquisition of the bedding warehouse in Market Passage and a depository in Mill Lane, followed in 1894 by property at 10,Market Street and in 1896 by property at 38, Sidney Street.

The development was not without its problems. Another hand written letter to all staff in January, 1894 said that for the first time since its formation the company business had shown a "very marked decrease." For the first nine months of the year the "returns were fairly maintained, but October and November compared very unfavourably with the same months in 1892, while in December every department suffered severely from the general depression."

It said the board relied upon their staff to endeavour during the present year by increased attention and greater care to arrest the decline. It added the company had escaped with but few bad debts and in consequence of that and a somewhat lessened trade expenses account, the board intended to distribute the annual bonus.

The store seems to have taken the training of its staff very seriously, particularly the apprentices who spent long hours learning their craft, and were expected to know the qualities of materials used in all the departments they worked. There was also a strict discipline with severe recriminations should any staff be caught stealing or breaking the house rules. Salaries were poor, but pretty much in line with other shops in Cambridge and other towns. Apprentices and juniors might only receive amounts as small at £10 to £15 a year, although an experienced salesman could expect to earn upwards of £60 or £70 a year, with the salaries usually paid monthly in arrears. The annual bonus was a vital ingredient. Some staff still lived in and their meals were provided. An example of wages at the lower level was confirmed in September, 1895 when W.I. Moody entered the employment of Eaden Lilley as a clerk at a wage of 14 shillings per week - plus tea.

Holidays and sick leave were unpaid until the end of 1895, but the board tended to make financial concessions to those who had been with the store a while, and were taken ill. Help was also given from time to time to staff who were convalescing after an illness or operation. By Christmas 1895 the directors had embarked on some pretty advance practices for looking after staff that were taken ill. Firstly they appointed two "medical men", and sick staff were referred to them first, without cost. Secondly they agreed to pay a full salary for employees who were off sick up to one month; although the staff involved were to have their bonuses reduced according to the length of time they were away sick. In January 1896 the firm set up an account with bankers Messrs Mortlocks under the heading Medical Aid and Rest Fund so that staff needing holidays after sickness could be paid.

It seems fairly clear that the board were anxious to retain senior and experienced staff and reflected that view in salary and perks. There was a reasonable turnover of staff, some switching to other retail outlets and some changing careers, which was not so easy.

There were, however, plenty of newcomers waiting to join the staff at the store, and to work in an industry which offered security and regularity if not high salaries. Security was a major concern for many families, and it became an important aspect of Victorian life, particularly for the working classes, where the sudden loss of an income could bring dramatic problems for the family. True, a single person could probably scrape by on £1 or £2 a week. but it wasn't easy, and certainly wasn't easy for large families who needed every available penny to keep their homes ticking over. The reliability of a family member working at Eaden Lilley, earning a fixed sum, plus a bonus and being rewarded with the prospect of promotion, was a mighty comfort for many families in Cambridge.

Staff were required to abide by firm rules during their employment, including an agreement described as "almost feudal" by one historian, the vexed question of applying to the board to marry. There were, no doubt, some traditional reasons for the moves, and there was clearly an attempt to stop financial over-commitment by some employees, but for the staff employed in 1894 it must have been a constant source of discussion and probably even resentment.

The fact that the application had to be made in the first place was no doubt tiresome, but to be refused permission to marry must have been a bitter blow to potential bride and groom.

In November, 1894 the board was particularly high-handed in its dealings with one F.Jones, who worked in the oil shop. He had found and wooed his lady in the few hours when he wasn't working and they had planned a Christmas wedding. Instead of offering congratulations and approval the board moaned that they had "noted his intention but should have preferred that the matter should have remained in abeyance until the financial year had ended."

There were a variety of other examples of the company ruling the life of employees, not least a problem with employee W.Parker who had apparently bought a house in Maids Causeway which, in the opinion of the directors was "above his needs and beyond his means."

In January 1896 they told him they were unhappy with the situation, that they took a serious view of the "extreme unwisdom of his act" and required him to resign his position. The poor man quickly saw the error of his ways and made a "strong plea for the retention of his situation" throughout the year so that his son's education might be completed. The directors eventually agreed to this request and a letter from Parker dated January 25, of that year showed a new address - 6,Causeway - and agreed to the terms of £180 per annum, with no bonus, payable monthly. The arrangement was to end on December 31, 1896.

These moves, outrageous by today's standards, were considered perfectly normal in the Victorian era where there were clearly defined rules and where class distinction was uppermost. Family run business was clearly middle class, below society by birth and inheritance, but a long way above working class which was also split into its own levels.

In Bleak House (1) Charles Dickens wrote:-

> There is a salaried clerk who devotes the major part of his thirty-shillings a week to his personal pleasure and adornment, repairs half price to the Adelphi at least three times a week, dissipates majestically at the cider cellar afterwards, and is a dirty caricature of the fashion which expired six months ago.
>
> There is the middle-aged copying clerk, with a large family,who is always shabby, and often drunk. And there are the office lads in their first surtouts, who feel a befitting contempt for boys at day schools, club as they go home at night, for saveloys and porter, and think there's nothing like 'life.'

And in the Cambridge Social History of Britain (2) a clear picture of middle class attitudes is painted by Leonore Davidoff who comments:-

> Provincial and nonconformist backgrounds had barred many in the middling ranks from political and social power. For them, in particular, the family had become a vital resource. They indefatigably advocated familial forms for all institutions except those that were intended to punish, control or harden by their specifically non-familial structure: workhouses, hospitals barracks and boys' public schools. In their doctrine, simply living a solid domestic existence became an act of patriotism and class reconciliation.

All this combined to make a series of work ethics and domestic rules where everyone knew "their station" in life, and employers required their staff to stay within their class, an attitude which lasted until after the First World War.

Early in 1894 the company had acquired the front shop of 10, Market Street which it intended to use as a furniture showroom, and the house on the premises was rented out at £65 a year.

By now Eaden Lilley was employing a total of 114, and the holiday list for that year shows some family names that were to stay with the company for many years ahead. They included Mack, Heath, Rutt and Kirkup. It also showed that the store could boast departments handling linens, dresses, haberdashery, hosiery, carpets, wholesale, millinery and the oil shop. The staff included six upholsterers, three vanmen, four polishers and seven carpenters.

The following year acquisition of new premises seems to have given way to improving the facilities and equipment that Eaden Lilley already held. A platform weighing machine, acquired from the famous Avery company, replaced the existing scales in the Oil Shop warehouse, a room in the Feather place in Market Passage was turned into a French polishers shop, and gasfires replaced open fireplaces in the dressmaking work room. Gas meters, a "slow combustion stove", wires for "carrying fire brigade calls", fire hydrants and a host of other minor improvements were made during the year.

There were also improvements in Cambridge itself that year, although slightly more expensive. A mains drainage system was constructed at a cost of £150,000 - previously the river had carried all drainage away from the town. Eaden Lilley connected 12 and 23 Market Street to the system in March, 1897

A major contract was confirmed for the supply by the store of 5000 dozen candles for Brimley, Wibley and Sons. It required an advance of 6d per dozen. The contract, with various changes in detail, was to remain with Eaden Lilley for several years

A short item, which was to have some long term importance for the company, was noted in the board meeting minutes for May 13, 1895, which recorded Walter Eaden Lilley, then aged 21, had entered the business and would be working under A.J. Mack in the wholesale department.

By 1896 property at 38, Sidney Street had been acquired and was used as a cabinet furniture warehouse, and the remainder rented out for accommodation.

The annual day out, attended by a total of 145, including the directors, was taken at Great Yarmouth in July, 1896. The amount of food provided seems substantial, but as about a third of the average working class income was spent on food in those days, perhaps the total consumed was not too great. It consisted of a "supply of light refreshments" on their train journey to Great Yarmouth, a "splendid dinner" at mid-day and tea in the town. There was also food on the journey home.

To a large extent the late 1890s were the golden days of the British Empire and Imperial expansion; there was a feeling of greatness, and although employees may not have seen big benefits the security of companies like Eaden Lilley were of paramount importance. New lands for the empire, "on which the sun never sets" also meant major export opportunities and the import of materials and products including cotton, hardwood, cocoa and raw materials for soap, cans and even bicycles which had found substantial favour in Cambridge. Eaden Lilley found itself providing bicycles - a bit like company cars - for some of its employees or paying an allowance for "wear and tear" of £3 a year to staff members like A.J. Mack and C.L.Rudd.

A constant series of minor, and sometimes not so minor, changes were being made with the properties under control of the company.

Lengthy negotiations were held with neighbours and the local authorities as the directors sought more space for their expanding operations, particularly with extra storage space required for warehousing. The search for bigger premises continued although it was still to be many more years before the first full blown reconstruction of the store took place.

The silver salver presentation to William Eaden Lilley in February, 1897
was commemorated and "much prized" by the family.

Back after the short Christmas break in 1896 the staff were met with firm guidelines on hours and work conditions. Work, they were told, started at 8.00am "sharp" with 10 minutes for lunch, one hour for dinner and 30 minutes for tea, with "work to cease not before 7.00pm"

Employees should not take on outside work while in full employ with the company, and staff in the Upholsterers Shop were warned about noisy behaviour.

Whatever the ups and downs of life as a worker at the company there seems little doubt that they held the head of their company in high regard. A surprise presentation was made to William Eaden Lilley in February 1897, of a silver salver, as "a mark of esteem and affection" by the employees of the company. The original plan was that only the heads of departments should contribute to the salver, but, reported a local paper, "so general was the desire to do honour to Mr Lilley that it was decided to extend the list and all in the employ of the company contributed." The salver was accompanied by an illuminated address, which despite the flowery language, did seem to genuinely reflect the views of the employees.

It said:-

> *We the undersigned desire most respectfully to tabulate our expression of kindly regard for your kindness, sympathy and generous concern for our wellbeing. We ask your acceptance of the accompanying salver as a remembrance of the happy relations existing between employer and employee. It is our hearty wish that you may long be spared amongst us, and your future life fraught with that which shall contribute to your highest good, also that you may continue to exercise that personal supervision of the great interest of the business which we all have at heart.*

Fifty years of Queen Victoria's reign was celebrated in June 1887 with a thanksgiving service in Westminster Abbey. She declined to wear the crown and robes of state, but instead appeared in black as a constant reminder of the death more than 25 years earlier of Prince Albert. In line with thousands of other companies around the country Eaden Lilley provided some monies - a total of £50 - towards the Golden Jubilee Fund.

The company also allowed some time off for employees anxious to join the local Volunteer Corps, some parts of which were to be involved in the Boer Wars.

The wars were fought between the British and the Dutch settlers, the Boers, in South Africa, with the major conflicts between the autumn of 1899 and January 1900. A series of Boer successes led to several British garrisons being besieged including those at Ladysmith and Mafeking. British counter attacks under Lord Roberts led to the relief of the garrisons, and wild excitement gripped the British public as the news was received in the UK.

Cambridge, like most other towns, celebrated with bonfires, fireworks, flags and drink. The second issue of the Cambridge Graphic, "an illustrated journal of town. county and university life" published in May, 1900 devoted pages to the celebrations on the Relief of Mafeking, which reported "there was no point at which it was possible to place a flag at which a flag was not placed." It said people, horses and bicycles wore the colours of the day." It estimated that some 20,000 spectators attended the bonfire, including about 2,000 undergraduates. There was, said the newspaper, plenty of boisterous behaviour, plenty of drinking but little drunkeness.

The newspaper is also interesting from the advertisements it carried, although none from Eaden Lilley. Fashion and household furniture, menswear and bicycles figured large in the columns. The Conduit coat for men, costing from three guineas, was advertised by Hewish sporting tailor in King's Parade; the "gold medal" Eagle range was being sold by A.Macintosh & Sons of Market Place; "smartest hats, toques and bonnets" were being sold by May Millinery of The Cury; "artistic gowns" were advertised by George Stace of The Cury and Robert Sayle & Co were offering silks, dresses. costumes, millinery, mantles, furs, linens, carpets, furnishing, hosiery, drapery and gloves.

As the new century dawned Eaden Lilley was finding itself with some tough competition, but the years ahead were to show that it was equal to the challenge.

The life of an apprentice was not intended to be fun, and in the early 1930s the straight-laced department heads at Eaden Lilley made a point of sticking to that basic rule.

For 17-year-old Aubrey Fewell, and the other five apprentice boys in the store it was hard to find a moment of light relief. They started work at 8.00am and worked through until 5.30pm, all for the sum of £10 a year for the first year, £15 for the second year and £20 for the third year.

Keeping the store in prestine condition was a requirement, and apprentices were expected to take their share of the load. The shoe department in 1928

First task each day was to sweep the floors, which were carefully checked by the supervisors before breakfast at 8.30am, a moment of brilliant relief for the youngsters, bacon and eggs followed by marmalade and toast. Even that had its problems when Aubrey Fewell blotted his copybook by adding mustard to the marmalade of the senior apprentice. The kitchen staff reported the terrible deed and he was given a severe wigging by a director.

The rest of the day was spent cleaning, carrying, helping and running errands for the senior staff, acting as a junior shop assistant and shadowing the work of more senior staff.

"It was a pretty good firm, but it was a miserable life for the apprentices; there was not much joy among the department heads, who seemed to find it extremely difficult to laugh about anything.

"It was a regimented society, a very formal atmosphere, everything had to be just right."

Despite that the apprentices found amusement. "The fun was getting round the system," says Aubrey Fewell.

The Lilley family were good employers who took an active interest in their staff, but "below stairs" a different set of rules applied.

The apprenticeship required a year in the blind department, a year in the curtain department, and a final year in the carpet department. "We were dealing with customers fairly quickly, but we were carefully supervised."

Despite the difficult times he did manage to catch the eye of an attractive young lady in the soft furnishing offices, and used every opportunity to visit that section of the store. He also joined the tennis club where the lady was a member.

Apprenticeship over, the 20-year-old could not wait to quit the company and headed up to London eventually working at Bentalls of Kingston.

War service saw him with the Royal Corps of Signals serving in Africa and Italy. After the war, by now married to Eva, the girl from soft furnishings, he went back to work in London, but by the early 1950s they were both back in Cambridge and both working at Eaden Lilley. For many years they had a company flat, living above the nanny to the Lilley family.

He had applied for an advertised vacancy in the bedding department, and after an interview with Kenneth Lilley he was back with his old company.

After a short while he took over as bedding buyer, and by the time he had retired in 1981 he was also the buyer for the linen department.

"In those days we were called buyer-managers. The job involved visiting factories and checking the products, and the watchword was 'value for money'.

'We were certainly not the cheapest in Cambridge, but Kenneth Lilley was extremely anxious to make sure we gave the best value."

A lot of beds and mattresses were supplied to colleges, and the hospitals in the region.

When he took over the department its annual turnover was about £10,000. By the time he retired it had risen to £250,000

The career of Eva Starmes really took off in 1927 when the company discovered that the person they had employed to act as switchboard operator could not hear ! Eva, who had been working as a cashier in the store was asked to take over the role.

She had left school at 16 with good qualifications and high hopes of a job in a solicitor's office, but there were no vacancies and so she took the cashiers job at 8/- a week with Eaden Lilley. She ran a small cubicle where shop assistants from several counters would arrive with bills and customers' money. She would sort out change and receipts, hand back both to the shop assistant who would then return the goods, change and receipt to the customer.

"It seems remarkably old fashioned now, but in those days I think it was considered pretty advanced," recalls Eva.

As switchboard operator for Cambridge 1234 she had to connect customers with departments, or inter-connect departments by using a series of wires and plugs on a large and complicated switchboard. Most of the calls were internal; in 1928 few homes in Cambridge had telephones. The switchboard was housed at 7, Market Street, and the company only employed one telephonist.

She later moved into the main office, and helped type invoices for all departments. An important move came when she was switched to work as secretary for Archibald Mack, buyer in the soft furnishing and carpets department, which also used to hire out items like prints, chairs and coverings for major events in Cambridge.

On their return to Cambridge in the 1950s Eva Fewell ran the furniture office, but when the department moved into the main store, she was switched and helped organise and run the removal department. At that stage the store ran four vehicles specifically for the removal business. She retired aged 70.

SHOW ROOM

12   W. EADEN LILLEY & C° LIMI

Chapter 5

High standards
and high quality

The continued development of the railway system at the end of the 19th century and start of the 20th century, combined with expansion plans by Eaden Lilley, led to the demand for more workers - but this time of the four legged variety.

Cambridge clattered to the shoes of a variety of horses as they drew four-wheeled closed vans, Spring-carts, drays, low-loading floaters, hansom cabs, broughams, buses, charabanc, hearses that also doubled as hospital transport, and the ubiquitous two wheeled floats mounted on cranked axles used by milkmen, butchers and traders involved in house to house deliveries.

Vanmen, their "mates" and helpers, were in particular demand among the stores, shops and companies that provided services for their customers in and around the town.

And there was a constant need for the four legged workers who literally provided the horsepower for the transport. With the meticulous requirement that you would expect for the era, someone had the task of detailing all the animals that were acquired by Eaden Lilley over more than 20 years, the price paid, and what happened to the workers after they had completed their tour of duty with the store.

The first in the carefully preserved beige coloured book, simply titled "Horses", although not the first to be bought by the company, was a six- year-old grey mare, actually named "Grey Mare." She boasted a height of 15.1 hands, and arrived in the company stables in September, 1891, having been bought from Barker at Over for £45. Having spent 11 years with Eaden Lilley she was sold back to the same man in 1902 - this time for £8.

The years 1899 and 1900 saw seven new horses, nearly all bays, and responding, or perhaps not, to names including Flying Fox, Kitty, Springer and Diamond. They were aged five or six and bought for prices ranging from £35 to £43. Local farmers or dealers appeared to be the main source and the horses ranged in height from 15.1 hands to 16 hands.

Eaden Lilley's demands for horses were relatively small compared to say the railways, which required thousands of horses and carts for parcel deliveries around the country, but nonetheless the store had a booming little delivery business, needed the animals for collecting supplies including those from warehouses, and used the horse-drawn vehicle as we would use a van or lorry today.

Another section of the book deals with the time some of the animals spent out at grass, the feeds required by some horses, and a list of drivers in the Horse Parades of 1910, 1911,1912 and 1913. As we have already seen, long term employment was often the order of the day and drivers like Chandler, Clark, Phillips, Thurlow and Nightingale figured in most parades.

A small section of the book referred to accidents, although that seems to have been dropped after a while. There is a reference to an accident in May, 1907 when an Eaden Lilley horse, Pilot, fell in Barton Road and broke its knees, and the shafts of the vehicle.

The contingencies of war also make for sad reading. Several horses were called up in 1914 including the light brown mare Judy who was bought aged five in 1908 for £46, and sold to the government "for war" six years later for £45. She was joined by an unnamed bay, a chestnut named Ginger, and the 16.2h gelding Charger, appropriately named for military duties.

Sophisticated transport for van drivers and commercial travellers at the company in 1911

Most of the animals that spent their time at Eaden Lilley seemed to have lived uncomplicated lives, and nearly all were sold on. At least one died from blood poisoning and two were reported killed, but the high standard of care shown by the store to its horses is well recorded and the longevity of their employment certainly reflects that attention.

The early years of the 20th century brought a level of calmness, security and peace to Britain and its major towns like Cambridge, and allowed the business of creating business to forge ahead. Apart from the advent of the internal combustion engine, which was soon to develop its own force in the world, there was a certain peace and regularity to life, and the citizens of town and country carried on with their lives under Edward VII, who was 60-years-old when he succeeded Queen Victoria.

The financial situation at W.Eaden Lilley and Company, which will not figure large in this book, was showing a steady upward curve in many areas, and was no doubt a source of comfort to the directors and employees of the store. Turnover, for instance, in 1901 was £148,592, and gross profit was £33,966. By 1903 the turnover was £153,119 and gross profit £37,445. By 1907 turnover was £155,204 with a gross profit of £37,608, and so it continued through the early 1900s and even through the Great War, with a turnover in 1918 of £342,780 and a gross profit of £66,055.

If there was a concern it was undoubtedly over the lack of suitable property, and the company regularly embarked on sorties into the local area to see whether premises could be acquired to help with its expansion. In 1906 it acquired 5 and 6, Market Passage, and in 1907 it included 7,Market Street in its portfolio.

Stacked floor to ceiling, the wholesale department at Eaden Lilley in the early 1900s.

A beautifully illustrated furniture brochure was published by the company about this time which proclaimed its telegraphic address, and its telephone number, which was 13. It also listed its departments as general drapery stores at 12, Market Street; ladies outfitting at 7, Market Street; fancy silver goods, pictures and picture framing, travelling bags and trunks, fancy leather goods, and more at 10, Market Street; oil, colour and brush department at 12, Market Street; carpet, floorcloth, linoleum and soft furnishing department at 23, Market Street; bedstead and bedding showrooms in Market Passage; hardware at 5 and 6 Market Passage; perambulators, mail carts, sewing machines, wicker chairs, folding screens and more as "under Henry Martyn Hall"; cabinet furniture warehouse at 38, Sidney Street; bedding factory and warehouses at Mill Lane and carpet beating and cleaning at Saxon Road.

The brochure said that the extensive showrooms and galleries were "constantly being replenished with new goods of the latest styles." It also offered a free delivery service in town and within a radius of 15 miles for orders of more than £10.

Prices make interesting reading with feather pillows selling at 2/3d, double woven spring mattresses at 13/-, blinds from 3/9d and cork carpet, "specially recommended for nurseries, corridors and landings" at prices between 1/11d to 3/3d per square yard.

The furniture range was substantial including a 3ft carved oak bureau at £5-10/0d; 12ft by 4ft 6in carved oak extending dining table at £14-1/6d; a 6ft walnut sideboard with shield shaped mirror and copper mountings at £18-18/0d; a stained walnut suite in "Saddlebags and velvet, comprising couch, two easys and four small chairs" at £6-15/0d; an inlaid mahogany cabinet at 11 guineas; an inlaid bureau Sheraton style from £3-10/0d; a mahogany bedroom suite, "Adams" style comprising wardrobe, dressing table, washstand with marble top and back and three chairs for 32 guineas, and an Alexander baby chair, adjustable to four different positions for 13/6d.

Whichever department they visited customers expected, and received, high standards of service, and in the background there were continued efforts to make sure the standards were maintained. A 1903 rule book for all staff included the following:-

* *"Serve customers in turn; when necessary serve two at a time.*

* *"Avoid pressing customers to have small parcels sent containing fragile materials.*

* *"Never conceal a defect or damage in any goods because the customer does not notice it or to think to ask if it is perfect.........If a customer is deceived or disappointed through having goods misrepresented, the firm will compensate the customer, and hold the assistant responsible for one half of the loss."*

And on general matters the rules included:-

* *"Waste of time in the lavatory and W.C. will be deemed a serious offence."*

* *"Assistants to pay for goods lost, soiled or damaged through their carelessness, and such goods to be charged at cost."*

* *"Attention is drawn to the necessity of coming to business with clean hands, clean boots, shirts, collars etc. Rings, flowers and other showy ornaments are discountenanced. Gossiping, standing in groups or lounging about in an unbusiness-like manner is expressly forbidden. Reading newspapers or writing private letters during business hours is not allowed."*

The world was changing fast, but Eaden Lilley continued its path of high standards and high quality in a regular, well organised pattern which satisfied directors and staff, but more importantly, its customers. In the same year that the rule book was written the Wright brothers, at Kitty Hawk in the United States, made the first flight in a powered aircraft, and by 1909 Louis Bleriot had made the first flight across the English Channel. Within a few years machines that were not that different to the pioneers would be launching attacks against towns, cities and each other, some flown by youngsters from Cambridge.

A certain amount of tidying up of affairs took place within the company in May, 1908 at an extraordinary general meeting when the firm's Articles of Association were altered under the heading "capital" where it was resolved that "no invitation shall be made to the public to subscribe for any shares or debentures of the company" and that no shares could be transferred without the previous written consent of the board. The special resolution was confirmed and signed by company secretary Frederick Deen Pryor.

By 1911 the network of property in and around Market Street had been increased with the acquisition of numbers 19 and 20, which was later turned into the blankets and household linen department.

As we have seen, Walter Eaden Lilley joined the company is 1895 and worked his way through departments as he built up a knowledge of the business. In June 1898 four board members, Philip Henry Lilley, Edward Moore, Alfred Charles Mansfield and Frederick Pryor wrote to the Eaden Lilley chairman suggesting that Walter be made a director. Their letter said: "His presence at our board meetings should prove of great assistance to him in attaining that general acquaintance with the many details of our business which is so essential to those concerned in its government, and he would also have an opportunity of testing the value of the methods by which the cordial relations between employer and employed have been for so many years so happily maintained, and which we feel sure you earnestly desire should be confirmed in the future.

"We need hardly add that it will give us all great pleasure individually to assist him as far as lies in our power."

The training and assistance complete, his position on the board confirmed, Walter Eaden Lilley became the head of the company in 1912, aged 35 when his father retired. A year later his 72-year-old father died having given a lifetime to running and expanding the company which by now was in reasonable shape and looking to a future of further development.

Plans and hopes were sadly dashed in June 1914 with the assassination in Sarajevo of the Austrian Archduke Francis Ferdinand and his wife, an event which sparked the outbreak of the First World War. By August 4 Britain had declared war on Germany and the dreadful events of the next four and a half years were about to unfold.

Writing in the Cambridge Chronicle and University Journal's Armistice number in November 1918, Councillor A.R.Hill reflected on the summer of 1914:-

> At Cambridge things had gone on as usual, and we had settled down to the customary relaxation of the Long Vacation with never a thought of the coming trouble. We had been concerned, it is true, but certainly not disturbed, at the murder of the Archduke, and the political unrest on the Continent, and men and women carried out their holiday arrangements without hesitation, scattering themselves over the face of the earth and water as was the Cambridge way up until the year of the great break. Some of our residents travelled as far as the Antipodes.........and hundreds distributed themselves about the Continent, all unheeding of the storm that was soon to burst. So things went on until the August Bank Holiday, the great festival of the Cambridge year, was almost upon us. Then vague disquiet began to manifest itself. The aggressiveness of the Central Empires was apparent, and a great European war was seen to be inevitable. The only matter in doubt was whether England would be able to keep out of it. By Saturday August 2 this had become less and less likely, and it was the one subject of discussion on Sunday (a day of brooding anxiety for thousands of people), and especially among our Territorials who had but just returned from their annual training.

The following day dawned the gloomiest Bank Holiday Cambridge had experienced.

Once the instructions to "mobilise" had been issued Cambridge was turned into a garrison town. Within days the Sixth Division was being based in the town, more and more volunteers were signing up, the Cambridgeshire Regiment carried out tours of the nearby villages enlisting extra soldiers, and students rushed back from vacation to join-up. Eaden Lilley workers were among the first to sign up, and many had previously become volunteers.

Troops poured into the town and the infantry set up a tented camp at Midsummer Common next to Jesus Grove, artillery was parked on Stourbridge Common; the cavalry occupied Long Common, howitzers and heavy field gun units were located on the Polo Ground at Trumpington, and almost every piece of green was occupied by khaki as town and country became a huge military camp.

By Monday September 7, wrote Councillor Hill, the troops had departed:-

> almost as suddenly as they had appeared amongst us, but not as silently, for the greater part of our population spent the night in the street watching their leaving. The scene will never be forgotten. All along the route men and women held out their hands to the marching troops, gifts were hastily thrust upon them, girls kept step alongside

their ranks, and tears and cheers commingled. For hours huge crowds hung about the railway enclosure in Tenison Road, from which a large part of the soldiers were entrained, and snatched last handshakes as the troop trains passed the crossing into the Midland Yard and they disappeared from view. Thus they went from us to the making of history and to become 'Mons Heroes'. By Tuesday morning all had vanished, leaving scarcely a trace of their occupation behind.

As the war progressed more volunteers took up arms from Cambridge, and in the early months it was notified to the Territorial Association that all the officers and 600 NCOs and men of the 1st Battalion of the Cambridgeshire Regiment had volunteered for foreign service. The offer was accepted and the battalion left for France in February, 1915.

After a lifetime of running and expanding the company the second William Eaden Lilley died, aged 72, in 1913

Wounded Belgians and refugees poured into the town and the former King's and Clare playing field was turned into a hutted hospital.

The town received a variety of formal visits including one from King George V who inspected the Welsh Division and the 11th Suffolks before they left for France. Queen Mary also visited the hospitals, General Smuts received an honorary degree and Lord Derby inspected troops and hospital facilities.

Many older Cambridge dons worked in government departments or as recruiting officers, as did some of the employees at Eaden Lilley.

It was not too long into the war before the long list of killed and wounded began to bring daily heartbreak to homes in Cambridgeshire; the county's own regiment suffering heavy casualties in France.

By 1917 the need for troops was replaced by the need for food, and home production was rapidly increased. Conscription for troops, which had not been much used in Cambridge, was replaced by conscription for industrial work, much being carried out by women. Later food coupons were issued.

The great fear of Zeppelin raids led to enormous precautions as we have seen in earlier chapters, although throughout the war no damage was caused by air raids. The best defence against night-time attacks was darkness, and shops and homes were subject to severe light restrictions.

Day after day, week after week the number of dead and injured rose. By war end in 1918 an estimated 850,000 British men had been killed and two million wounded. Officer training at public schools and universities meant young subalterns going straight to France to lead their men "over the top". The slaughter at this level was dreadful; about one in five graduates from Cambridge, for instance, were killed, and many more wounded.

It was only after the Armistice and eventual peace that the full horror of the war was revealed to a disbelieving population. It was to change the way of life, attitudes and beliefs almost overnight.

The Armistice issue of the Cambridge Chronicle gave its front page to an advertorial from Eaden Lilley. The headline exclaimed "The Armistice Signed - a just and lasting peace to follow."

It quoted Prime Minister David Lloyd George who had spoken at a Guildhall function where he said: "In this solemn moment of triumph - one of the greatest moments in the history of the world - in this great hour which rings in a new era, and the end of a colossal struggle, which is going to lift humanity to a higher plane of existence for the ages of the future, let us here and now own how much we are indebted to the valiant men who fought and endured so much that we should enter into this bright inheritance."

The company added: "The above sentiments so ably expressed by Mr Lloyd George indicate the feelings of gratitude which at this never to be forgotten moment all must feel to those who responded to the call of Duty and the claims of Right against Might."

It also thanked those men and women who had enabled the store to continue during the war years, it placed on record "our feeling of indebtedness to our customers for their forbearance during the long and trying ordeal", and it assured them of the company's utmost endeavour to retain customer confidence under the soon to prevail more normal conditions.

Most importantly it listed the nearly 170 staff members who over the four and a half years had joined the services or volunteered for work of national importance.

Eighteen names were listed In Memoriam. They were B.Chapman, C.Dunnett, H.G. Ellis, P.Hewitt, H.C.Le Grice, C.Lloyd, G.Mason, J.Mills, F.Muggleton, S.Mutimer, J.H.Marsh, J.Nightingale, S.Pike, A.S.Prime, A.D.Soames, D.J. Smith, B.Tabor and W.Tinworth.

Memories

A job for life

Shortly after the death of his father in 1939, 11-year-old Gordon Wilson found himself standing in front of "old Mr Mack" at Eaden Lilley's office in Market Street, and discussing whether he would care to follow in the family footsteps and join the firm.

However daunting the experience, the boy was calm enough to point out that he really rather preferred the idea of going into catering, and the old gentleman patted him on the shoulder and said, "Well, my boy, if you change your mind come and see me," and then pressed a half a crown into his hand.

Gordon Wilson had visited the store with his mother so that she could sort out her pension following the death of Horace Walter Wilson who was, for many years, foreman in charge of the removal department, and was one of the key members of the team involved in moving the Old University Library books. He was also one of the many store employees who saw service in the First World War and was taken prisoner in France where he contracted TB.

The 1939 meeting ended with Mrs Wilson being paid a pension of 10/- a week, which later rose to 15/- a week.

As fate would have it, when Gordon Wilson left school at 14, still in the middle of the Second World War, he decided he would be interested in a job with Eaden Lilley and after another interview started as an apprentice. And from the moment he joined the firm he decided that he would stay there for his working life, although he was a little concerned about the Dickensian conditions of the workshop in Sidney Street, and disenchanted with the 1/6d a week he received in wages.

His apprenticeship included periods in the cabinet shop, in the polishing shop, upholstery shop and in the bedding department where they made mattresses, and during the war, reconditioned second hand beds.

"The management took a great interest in their staff. If there were any problems, at home or work, they were there to help. They were true gentlemen employers, and we really did feel part of a family," he says.

Within a year he had transferred to the bedding and furniture departments as a trainee. His first job each morning was to light the slow combustion stove in a corner of the bedding department in Green Street, which was the only form of heating in the shop. There was little new for customers to buy and a lack of coupons slowed down the trade to a trickle.

His afternoons were spent in the large furniture department in Sidney Street which had four floors of furniture, largely second hand or reconditioned during the war years. Initially he was not allowed to speak to the customers, but later he was allowed to discuss the goods with customers and then pass on them on to sales assistant. Eventually he became a sales assistant.

Part of the company's removal fleet between the wars. Foreman Horace Walter Wilson is pictured, first left.

The demand during the war for mattress remaking was constant, and at one stage Eaden Lilley also had to put the work out to another firm. The mattresses were pre-war, and stuffed with hair, or flock - the coarse tufts and remains of wool or cotton. The mattresses were pulled to pieces and recovered as required, the hair or flock placed in a machine which removed all the dust, and then restuffed. Death bed mattresses were sent to a special sterilising plant in Cambridge before being remade.

Later in the war the old wooden bedsteads were partly replaced by utility furniture which was available in the store, subject to the right number of coupons.

Gordon Wilson's career progressed at a proper pace and he was made sales manager in the bedding department under buyer manager Aubrey Fewell. He took an early retirement package just one year ahead of his 50 years service with the firm.

12 W EADEN LILLEY & C° LIMI

Chapter 6

A task of "extraordinary interest"

It was the greatest library move ever, involving more than one million books, and was to engage W. Eaden Lilley & Co. Ltd, in one of its toughest jobs.

The contract to move the books from the Old University Library behind the Senate House in Cambridge to the New University Library in Queens Road had been won by the firm in early 1934, with plans to carry out the operation in the summer months.

It was in every sense a massive task and the store carried out a careful investigation as to how best make the move. The company decided against using the 11 motor vehicles they had, and instead planned to use horses and flat top trucks; a decision roundly criticised by the local press.

The scale of the task ahead of them was outlined by E.Ansell, the assistant university librarian when he gave a talk to staff members before the move.

Thomas Murkin (standing centre) worked as a foreman during the great library move. He is pictured with other workers taking a break between deliveries. The "snapshot" was taken by another employee, and a copy left with Thomas Murkin, who died aged 81 in November 1998.

"Your firm", he told them, "together with the library staff are awaiting a task of extraordinary interest, especially as no undertaking of this kind has ever been seen before in the library world. I feel sure we shall work in harmony, and we much look forward to the attainment of the end.

"One of the difficulties is that neither you, nor we, know how things will turn out, but after a few days at the job I expect we shall get into our stride and everything will go well."

The Old University Library had been built between 1837-42, although the formation of the library itself was probably around 1420. Every week scores of books were added to the collection until the building, designed by C.R.Cockerell, was heaving at the seams. After nearly 30 years of procrastination it was decided to build a new library on a new site. Architect Sir Giles Gilbert Scott presented his first sketch in 1931, and the building was complete by 1934. A £500,000 donation from the Rockefeller Fund had paid for the building, extra staff and the maintenance costs.

In his book The Buildings of England, Cambridgeshire, (1) author Sir Nikolaus Pevsner describes the new library as "a large symmetrical building of pale russet brick with a big central tower in axis with the new buildings of Clare College."

He adds that "an odd lack of decision goes through the whole design. The tower serves as a stock room of 12 storeys and is therefore slit open in vertical strips of windows. The same design is used for the wings on the left and right of the centre. But whereas this modern motif calls for a style of strict uprights and horizontals and a reduction of mass in the facades, the centre is mostly solid wall with a display of a giant arched entrance with rusticated surround."

These matters were probably of little concern to Eaden Lilley's staff whose main task was to fill the inside rather than debate the outside of the building.

Blessed by good weather they set about their task with the books being packed in special tea-chests, and loaded two high on the flat trucks. The horses did their work along the short journey and were unharnessed at the new library leaving the trucks to be unloaded as required. The horse then went back for another loaded truck.

The system was an undoubted success and allowed time for packing and unpacking, which was always carried out by the library staff.

The total move took nearly seven weeks, and according to records at the time "went very smoothly," encouraged by senior staff at the firm, and supported by "copious supplies of large jugs of tea for the men", provided by Mrs Anne Lilley.

Thomas Murkin of Barton Cambs, who worked in the joinery department at the company, was in charge of one of the gangs, many of whom were employed on a casual basis for the specific task. He recalled later that Eaden Lilley provided a uniform, plus aprons for the grand move.

The store had quite a reputation at the time for its removals, storage and packing operations carried out from 38, Sidney Street, from Market Street, Green Street, Mill Lane and Glisson Road. A carefully collected loose leaf booklet of "testimonials and suggestions" was prepared which detailed the three large buildings "specially constructed for the storage of furniture", which were well ventilated and centrally heated.

"Each consignment of furnishings is kept entirely to itself, separated from the lots belonging to other customers, but in such a way that there is always free ventilation."

The removal motors were described as "specially designed for this work and are on pneumatic tyres," and the removal staff had many years of experience of handling and packing valuable furniture.

The booklet provided some fascinating "removal hints," including:-

> *Clock pendulums should always be taken off and wrapped in paper with the keys and placed inside the clock or tied on the outside.*

> *Pictures should not be removed from the walls before the man arrives.*

> *Cutlery and steel or brass articles keep well if treated with Vaseline and wrapped in paper.*

> *Keys should either be collected before work starts, or tied to the handle or drawer or door. "This simple precaution will save considerable trouble and annoyance."*

> *"Eggs in isinglass should be taken out and packed in dry lime for removal for safe carriage, and on arrival at destination transferred to fresh isinglass."*

And on storage the firm offered a variety of tips including:-

> *Blankets, woollen articles and furs should be well shaken and then wrapped in brown paper, "which is impervious to moths. Pepper, camphor, insect powder, or other such preventatives can be used as an additional precaution."*

> *Preserves, pickles, oils, vinegar and other similar articles should not be stored. They may leak.*

> *Packages or boxes that may be required during storage should be marked "wanted."*

> *Carpets, rugs and felts are much better if beaten before being stored, and*

> *"on no account leave lucifer matches, cartridges, fireworks or paraffin among your effects."*

The between the wars economic roller-coaster that pushed Britain in and out of financial problems and unemployment, was ridden with some skill by the management at Eaden Lilley. Walter Eaden Lilley continued the paternalistic approach of his father with a rapidly expanding staff, and the company enlarged and developed under his careful guidance. By 1920 they had bought premises in Green Street which provided "landing docks" where five motor vans could be loaded and unloaded at the same time." A "Shopping in Cambridge" brochure a few years later said of the landing docks that "it is within the memory of some of the present staff, when one horse van only and one handcart were required for delivering goods and even then the van was in use during a part of each day only."

With typical astuteness the company managed to produce a booklet outlining the benefits and history of Eaden Lilley, but paid for by advertisements from other companies in the town. It was published to mark the 1928 reconstruction of the original premises at 12, Market Street. The development had extended the building to the back of numbers 13, 14 and 15 Market Street "thus creating one large store on a single site in addition to the several departments located at other addresses."

The business by this time included the sale of household goods and grocery, as well as drapery and complete house furnishing.

The writer of the foreword to the book was a little carried away with his description of Cambridge as "an aristocrat among English towns, but her appeal as a shopping centre is not to the few but to the many," although his intentions were clear enough - to pull more customers through the doors at Eaden Lilley.

"Shopping in Cambridge," he wrote, "is not so much a business as a social occupation of never-failing delight, for it has a permanent setting of the most romantic kind - a background of the richest architectural, historic and artistic interest.

"There is all the difference in the world between shopping amid such surroundings and among those of, say, one of the suburbs of a densely populated industrial city which seems to be the very symbol and expression of the commonplace and the mediocre."

He said that the House of Eaden Lilley has always been noted for the good quality of its merchandise, and retains a policy of service "which aims at giving complete satisfaction to every customer."

He then invites the reader on an extended tour of the store and its facilities. To avoid being churlish perhaps we should accept the invitation but take a shorter journey to look at what was on offer in the store in 1928-29.

The arcade was described as a "place of continual attraction for the lady shoppers." The window space had been increased by six

times the original area and "they are not just so much cubic space of storage room into which a proportion of the firm's stock is tightly packed; they are so arranged as to offer suggestions, to give an idea of colour and tone effects, of possible combinations of materials and shades, as well as a review of the latest styles and novelties in feminine dress."

A few years later Eaden Lilley display manager Henry Bates was to claim the title of "England's champion window dresser" and receive a cheque for £250 for his work in dressing a window with Heinz's products. Making the presentation Alderman P.J. Squires, president of the Cambridge Chamber of Commerce said that he thought Cambridge people should feel very gratified that "among all the thousands taking part, a local firm had managed to win the cup and cheque for £250." He described it as a remarkable piece of work.

Back with our guided tour we have found a second entrance nearer Market Hill which offers access to the grocery and confectionery department. The booklet lists the departments nearest the main entrance as ladies and gentlemen's hosiery, haberdashery and art needlework, art silk materials, woollen dress and cotton goods, with materials for blouses and lighter garments, together with fancy goods such as laces, ribbons, scarves, fur trimmings, gloves and umbrellas.

A montage of photographs taken from the Shopping in Cambridge booklet produced in 1928. They show the arcade, the stairs and well, and the household goods department.

"A large staircase of handsome design in mahogany and bronze leads from the ground floor to the first floor, on which are found the showrooms. In these, as elsewhere in the store, a point is made of displaying goods in such a way that people may walk round and inspect them at leisure."

The departments on that floor included ladies and children's outfitting, dressmaking, costumes, blouses, gowns, millinery and artificial silk underwear. Ladies were encouraged, in the millinery department, to try on as many models as they wanted in "quiet surroundings without the distraction of overcrowding or the general shop traffic."

The top floor was home to the staff dining rooms and rest rooms, "all of them spacious and airy."

The basement housed bargains, and at Christmas was turned into a toy department with a resident Father Christmas.

The remaining departments, bedding in Market Passage, furniture at Sidney Street, hardware and cutlery at 5 and 6, Market Passage, carpets, curtains and furnishing fabrics at 23, Market Street, blankets and household linen at 19 and 20, Market Street, had all been modernised and improved, and "show the comprehensive self-contained character of the business.

"The formerly complex problem of 'setting up housekeeping' involving separate expeditions to the premises of numerous firms, can now be carried through not only with less trouble and anxiety but with more pleasure and profit by calling W.Eaden Lilley & Co Ltd., into consultation, for at their premises can be obtained everything for the home."

The store, offering what today would be called "one-stop shopping" had the new telephone number of Cambridge 1234, and 30 extensions linking the various departments. There was also an out of hours number for the undertaking department.

The rapidly expanding company now had 400 employees, and a revised series of rules and regulations were published in 1932, which still required shop assistants to wear black boots and black dresses, and black or navy, or very dark grey suits.

The sales patter and approach was carefully outlined, and assistants were warned to "avoid asking unnecessary questions of customers before showing goods," and to "sell nothing on a misrepresentation." They were told that assistants should always be "attentive, polite, obliging and truthful to customers."

The 20-page booklet explained: "Every opportunity should be taken to introduce merchandise tactfully without forcing goods on a customer, but a tactful sales person can, by suggestion and recommendation, make much extra business and sell higher priced goods.

"N.B - Eighty sales people increasing their sales by only 2/6d per day for one year means an extra turnover of £3,000 and more profit available for bonus."

The assistants were urged to keep their counters tidy, and to cultivate the habit of doing everything rapidly and accurately. They should never address a lady as "Miss", but always "Madam", and should meet customers with a pleasant expression and give the impression they were pleased to see them, but avoid familiarity. "Remember that the whole organisation is judged by the one person with whom the customer comes into contact."

The rules and regulations detailed the hours worked, time given for meals, the bookwork that needed to be kept up to date, and a warning that "care and economy must be used in the use of paper, string, pins etc. Gas should be lowered, and the electric light turned off when not needed, and every endeavour be made to prevent waste of any kind."

One-stop shopping at the store included picture framing at 10, Market Street.

The autumn of 1932 saw the annual publication of the price list of groceries, oils, brushes, china, glass, cutlery and hardware. The firm's well known range of "Cambro" varnishes, paint, and enamel, "ground in our own mill" figured large in the brochure as did some of the most famous names of the day - some still around in the new millennium.

In the grocery and dry goods lists, adverts were taken by companies like Kiwi, and Cherry Blossom in boot polishes, Robinson's Barley, Crawford's biscuits, Huntley & Palmers ginger nuts, Carr's table water biscuits, Fry's milk chocolate, Bournville cocoa, Marmite, Homepride self-raising flour, Rowntree's cocoa, Chiver's jams, Peek Frean's, Bryant & May's matches, Libby's evaporated milk, Palmolive soap and Pan Yan pickle.

Prices included Daddies sauces at 9d a bottle, white pepper at 6d a quarter pound, meat pastes at 7d a jar, 2lb Empire jams in tins at 1/9, Heinz baked beans at 3d, Camp coffee at 10d, 1/7d or 3/9d a bottle, chocolate assorted biscuits at 2/2d per lb, Briskies, all British breakfast flakes at 8d, anchovy paste at 4d a jar, W.E.Lilley's own packet tea at 2/2 per lb, and, for the braver customer, castor oil at 2d a bottle.

In the kitchen utensils department meat safes made out of enamelled metal, were on sale with prices ranging from 10/6d to 18/6d; new patent whistling kettles at 2/3d for two pints, and housemaid's kneelers, gloves, boxes and steps at a variety of prices. There were also state of the art "new Crown Dandy rubber roller table top wringer with rollers" at £3.19/6, galvanised baths, coal scoops and coal hammers.

And if you wanted a good Christmas present for the lady of the house how about a new model Little Vesta sewing machine with enclosed gear or vibrating shuttle, prices from £3.19/6d to £6.10/0d.

The hardware side of the business had been largely established by George Heath, who joined the company in 1882, aged 14. His father, John Heath, had originally worked for the Lilley family in a variety of capacities including as a coachman, and went on to help buy and sell horses for the store. Even after his retirement he was called back to advise on the animals which were largely stabled in Mill Lane.

George Heath, who in later years became a company director, originally worked in the oil shop where large tanks of different oils were kept for lighting, engineering, heating and treating harness leather.

Director George Heath was largely responsible for establishing the hardware side of the store.

For many years the hardware department also mixed the Cambro paints referred to in the 1930s brochures.

Working his way up the scale George Heath eventually found himself responsible for the developing hardware department, together with crockery, grocery and sundries - soaps, detergents, starch etc.

At the same time the company ran a flourishing wholesale, which also fell under the direction of George Heath. One of the outside representatives for that department was Olaf Custerson, who joined the firm in 1939.

He recalls that there was little contact between the shop and the five representatives, apart from a Saturday morning meeting when George Heath and Miss Howlett would brief the reps on details of any new lines and prices that should be sold in the following week.

"We always found that the advice Mr Heath gave us was sound and helpful in selling these lines; his vast knowledge in the grocery and sundries trade was appreciated by the reps and the many shops we called upon over a large area."

The Second World War brought predictable problems for the reps including a savage reduction in the amount of petrol that could be used, and so they took to trains. One rep had to cover a very large area, from the Isle of Ely and the Fens, down to Downham Market, parts of Norfolk and large areas of Suffolk.

"The long train journeys, overnight stays and driving with masked headlamps during the winter months eventually proved too much for my colleague, and he decided to leave. I took over his area until my call up when I joined the RAF," says Olaf Custerson. His travels enabled him to discover an ideal spot to stay, with a Mr and Mrs George Lincoln who ran a general store, cafe, board and lodging bedrooms in Littleport near Ely. George Lincoln also ran a butcher's shop, so his guests were guaranteed good breakfasts and good evening meals.

A major problem for the reps was the need to carry large sums of money around.

Nearly all transactions were by cash, few shopkeepers had a bank account, and few small towns boasted a bank. The result was that until the Friday of each week - when the cash was handed over to an Eaden Lilley cashier-the reps could find themselves carrying as much as £600 in cash.

After his service in the RAF Olaf Custerson returned to Eaden Lilley in 1946, received a "welcome back" cheque, and took over a round from Alf Smith who had retired in his early 80s.

"Then I was back on the road, calling at shops in Cambridge and near villages, which was quite a change from the Fens," he recalls. "During the bad weather Alf used to wear short leather leggings, but I preferred Wellington boots."

The back-up and support from management and office staff was vital to the wholesale grocery operation, and involved a great deal of work and organisation especially during and immediately after rationing. Eaden Lilley's had to come up with a system that was fair to customers throughout the area.

"It had its difficult moments, but I thoroughly enjoyed my time with the wholesale department," says Olaf Custerson, who retired in 1974. "I well remember George Heath meeting me some Friday afternoons, after his retirement, and we would discuss what trade was like. Although well into his 80s he was very keen to hear how things were going."

As wholesaling became more competitive the company had to make a decision on its future involvement in the business. It became impractical to operate from Market Street and to buy a new building would have been very expensive. In the end the firm closed the wholesaling departments, and the reps, who also sold drapery, were found other jobs within the store.

George Heath had been appointed a director in July, 1934, and retired in 1954 after more than 70 years with the company. The board recorded his death in 1956 and the minutes noted that after entering the company as a junior "by dint of great appreciation and attention to business, he rose to become manager of four large departments which continually expanded under his able control." It said that after he was made a director he "continued to devote his whole energies to the well-being of the business."

The company suffered a substantial blow in 1934 when Walter Eaden Lilley, died suddenly at the early age of 57. Archibald J. Mack, who had carried out sterling work for the company was appointed managing director, and shortly after the war Walter's son Kenneth, born in 1911, was confirmed as governing director and then chairman, and his brother William Howard, was appointed deputy chairman.

The move to appoint Kenneth of West Road, Cambridge, as governing director was supported by the majority of the shareholders

Events will show that the decision to have the brothers effectively running the company was to have its problems as well as its advantages.

(1) The Buildings of England, Cambridgeshire, by Nikolaus Pevsner; published by Penguin, 1954.

Memories

A hard act to follow

At 21 newly married Ian Vernon had a tough decision to make; should he join the highly reputable Eaden Lilley at six guineas a week or should he take the £12 a week job with Marks and Spencers.

He and wife Joan spent a while considering the options. He had some experience in display work, had taken a correspondence course in the subject, but still needed more training. On the other hand nearly double the salary had great attractions particularly in the difficult period just after the Second World War.

There was, however, an added problem.

"In those days," he recalls, "if you worked for Marks and Spencers no one else would employ you. The trade looked down on the company; their reputation was very very low."

And so he decided to take the pay cut and go for the experience.

That was in 1948, and less than a year later he stepped into the shoes of the great Henry Bates, one time "England's champion window dresser", who had worked at the company for many years, but decided after the war that he needed a new challenge and left to run a chain of wool shops. Ian Vernon applied for the job, and after interviews with Kenneth and Howard Lilley was appointed display manager for the store on a six month basis - and given a rise of £50 a year.

"It was an interesting challenge, and a particularly tough act to follow," says Ian Vernon. His hopes of joining up during the war had been dashed by medical problems, and at one stage he had been told by doctors to "go home and make sure you take it easy."

Initially he was looking after 40 display windows, but within a short while that had been increased to 44 windows. After a while he had 10 display staff and two studio staff.

In the early days he and his team expected to change between 30 and 35 windows every week.

"I emphasised to my staff that we had to work as a team, although the buck was always going to stop with me."

Like all department heads he had to deal with staff problems from time to time, including the son of an RAF officer who had been expected to do extremely well. For the first week he worked very well, but then his attention and attendance dropped off. Eventually Ian Vernon found him taking drugs in an attic room at the store, which in the early 1950s was a relatively unusual event.

Each week the display manager would set out a window rota, and then discuss the matter with the sales director Howard Lilley to see if he had any particular ideas or items that he wanted displayed.

"We would then discuss the matter with the department buyers, who usually had different ideas on what was wanted, and eventually design a window around an agreed, or largely agreed, idea."

There was a major requirement for Ian Vernon, and to some extent Howard Lilley, to know what was in fashion and to make sure that the window concerned reflected the latest trend. That would entail, from time to time, visits to fashion shows in London, Zurich, Germany, Holland and Denmark and the World Exhibition in Brussels. There were also visits simply to look at window displays in stores around Europe.

"It was, and still is, very important to keep up with trends," he says.

The definition of a good window as far as Ian Vernon was concerned was its ability to sell. If it failed to do that it had failed in its prime objective.

An autumn window was dressed to include a china model draped in a black velvet skirt and a gold lame top. There was a certain interest in the material, but it was only when Ian Vernon went into hospital for an operation that he realised the success of the window dressing.

"One of the nurses told me she had seen the display and had bought the material and carefully made it into a skirt and top for the nurses annual ball. When she arrived at the function she discovered six other nurses in the same dress."

Window dressing is an ill-defined art.

"A lot of it depends on the imagination you can put into the window, to attract and encourage the customers. Like all things there is a knack, and sometimes it works, sometimes it doesn't."

And certain staff are good at certain subjects. Perhaps a window dresser is first class at hardware, but poor at fashion, another good at shoes and hopeless at furniture.

Over the years Ian Vernon became involved in shopfitting, and later the lay-out of floors and alterations, and gradually he acquired a vital knowledge of fixtures and fittings, including the revenue to be earned from the available space.

Chapter 7

No news is good news

In the dreadful times the people of Britain show a remarkable ability to unite against the common enemy. The awful events of September,1939 when Germany overran Poland in just four weeks and ignited the flames of the Second World War, welded the British together for six years as they staggered through the agonies of a vast global conflict.

Although many parts of Britain escaped the Luftwaffe bombing and direct action, no part of the country escaped an involvement in the war, or its hardships. Britain's determination to stand firm was the talk of the free world, and the envy of some countries who had quickly capitulated to the aggressor.

A day out for senior management, (left to right) company secretary R.B. Horne, Howard Lilley, George Heath and Kenneth Lilley.

Despite such a short gap between the Great War and Hitler's invasion of Poland, there was no lack of volunteers for the services. Towns and villages across the country provided men and women for the forces or "work of national importance." Cambridge did more than its fair share and Eaden Lilley was able to report that "the staff have responded loyally to the country's call" with 95 men and 45 women of the pre-war staff joining up.

The Cambridgeshire Regiment, which became part of the Suffolk Regiment at the outbreak of war, saw service in the Far East until the surrender in Singapore in 1942.

Industry adapted to the new demands of war and Marshalls of Cambridge, for instance, found itself repairing and converting aircraft. It was bombed twice, without loss of life and with limited damage to some aircraft.

The Home Front had its own problems with rationing, severe shortages and little money for families to live on; the wife of a private soldier with two children had just over 30/- a week. "Where necessary" Eaden Lilley provided allowances to the wives of married members serving in the forces.

The company's annual report presented to the shareholders on March 20,1943 showed a net profit of £11,906, but the directors - A.J.Mack, G.Heath, K.Lilley, W.H.Lilley and R.B.Horne, who was also the company secretary - were in pessimistic mood. They warned it had been "one of the most difficult in the history of the company", and that staff difficulties had been extremely harassing, and "the never ending regulations which reach us from all quarters necessitate considerable thought and planning to maintain the smooth flow of business."

On top of that there was little money around and few goods to buy, threatening another tough year ahead.

"There is no doubt that the quantity of manufactured goods now available in the country is considerably less than last year and the severity of the clothing rationing is most marked. In consequence it is considered that we cannot hope to maintain the turnover of the past few years and a serious drop is anticipated.

"No opportunity, however, is neglected to obtain saleable non-couponed goods and every effort will be made to serve the public and to maintain the reputation of the firm."

Profits were helped a little by a decrease in expenses; a smaller staff, little spent on repairs because of restrictions, a reduction in War Risk Insurance premiums, and "almost every item of expense has, to some extent, decreased." Even expenses for running the ARP (Air Raid Precautions) branch had been negligible. In previous years this has been a particular burden with government requirements for the provision of a 10,000 gallon water tank and motor pump. Also part of the top floor of the Market Street premises had been given over to Ministry of Labour Women's Section for the duration of the war.

The company also provided two vans, which were converted into ambulances for use by the ARP. They were stationed at No 4 First Aid Depot, which was based in the heavily sandbagged St Paul's School in Russell Street, Cambridge. Each held four stretchers. One was driven by H.E.Fisher who remembers that the vehicles were used during bombing raids on the town including Vicarage Terrace and Hills Road. Casualties were taken to the Old Addenbrookes Hospital in Trumpington Street. "They never let us down," he says.

Serving officers on leave appear to have made a point of settling their accounts at Eaden Lilley during 1943, for reasons that can only be guessed at, and for the first time the Bad Debts Account was in credit.

Some companies, and some individuals for that matter, made fortunes out of the war, but most did not. It is probably fair to say that Eaden Lilley ticked along with acceptable profits in one or two years. Like thousands of other firms in the UK the war had come as a hefty blow at a time when things were looking good.

Between the wars and under the quiet leadership of Walter Eaden Lilley, it had expanded considerably and remodelled bringing a lot of its departments under one roof and offering a full range of services to its enthusiastic customers. It is, perhaps, easy to overlook the stability provided by the chairman before he died in 1934. His obituaries referred to him as having a "retiring disposition", and although he was not a prominent figure in the public life of Cambridge he was "known both in business and social service circles for his kindness and practical sympathy." A one time director of the Cambridge Permanent Benefit Building Society, he was also on the general committee of Addenbrooke's Hospital, and worked with the Cambridgeshire Society for the Blind, and was an enthusiastic supporter of the Emmanuel Congregational Church. He ran a farm at Grantchester on "progressive lines." One local paper obituary commented: "he had the welfare of the whole staff of Eaden Lilley & Co always at heart, while not only employees but others enjoyed the hospitality of his seaside home at Hunstanton."

The vast bulk of his estate of £164,778 went to his wife Annie with monies to his sons and daughters.

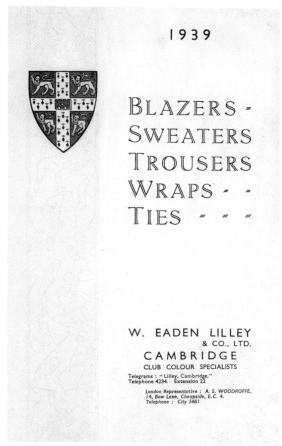

The company developed a fine reputation for providing blazers, sweaters, wraps and ties.

The staff at Eaden Lilley, who often referred to themselves as part of a large family, clearly approached the war years as one body. They supported and helped each other, kept in touch with their members who served in almost every theatre of war and in all three services. The memory of that support, from both company and staff, stayed with all those who survived the conflict.

Six months before the outbreak of war the senior executives had been busy sorting out insurance problems and costs, and were looking to replace a Grinnell sprinkler system for the whole store, which was likely to cost a substantial £1,500. They also compiled a most detailed report, running to dozens of pages, on the fixtures and fittings within the company, even down to lino, blinds and wall fittings.It totalled just over £11,500.

The company had, by now, developed a fine reputation for providing blazers, sweaters, trousers, wraps and ties. It provided coverage for much of the UK, and in blazers alone offered university, old boys', club and regimental badges. The pre-war list of old boys' blazers, "with cloth that is in stock" included Bancroft, Blundell, Chigwell, Eton, Felsted, Harrow, Haberdashers, Lancing, Malvern, Oundle, Rugby, Radley, Westminster, Wellington and Wrekin. Regimental blazers, up to 32/6d plus 10/- or 12/- for the wire badge, included the Royal Air Force, Royal Flying Corps, Royal Tank Corps, Royal Artillery, Royal Naval Air Service and the Brigade of Guards. Clubs included those at Oxford and Cambridge, Midland Bank, Guy's Hospital and the Civil Service Sports Club. The full range of colleges was also included in the list. The department also produced school and club blazers to order, and made up in the cloth and colour "that your club committee wish to see, before placing their order."

A separate list of badges was also provided for colleges, schools and clubs in the UK and regiments around the Empire.

The department was also tapping in to the "increasing popularity of crested ties" which it described as remarkable. In later years it was to offer one of the finest collections of embroidered ties in the world.

By September, 1939 the threat of war had been hanging over the country for some 18 months, and gas masks had been issued to a population fearful of poison gas attacks from the air; ARP units had been set up; National Service Handbooks issued to every household, and black-out precautions started. The eventual announcement by Prime Minister Neville Chamberlain that Britain and France were at war with Germany was largely treated with a dreadful resignation.

The Eaden Lilley volunteers saw service around the globe. They served in the Army, the Royal Navy and the Royal Air Force. Many returned to the firm after the war, received a "welcome back" cheque and then got on with their lives in a job that had been held open or recreated for them. The family of Eaden Lilley was almost intact again.

Some of the volunteers, however, did not return.

On the return to peacetime trading the company continued to jog along as if nothing very much had happened.

Helped by the absence in the city of other retail players, with the exception of the John Lewis Partnership store, Robert Sayle, it was able to do so without really trying too hard. In addition, and very significantly, there was a complete absence of any serious profit motive. Furthermore, a fundamental reluctance on the part of the chairman to make any changes - much less take any risks - was to prove a serious impediment to the company's further development.

Against this background the store was allowed to stagnate when it should have been embarking on a continuing upgrading and updating process to keep abreast of rapidly changing modern merchandising methods and more exciting presentations.

At about this time Eaden Lilley joined the Independent Stores Association. As the name suggests this was a group of independent department stores located across the length and breadth of the UK, which had got together to compare notes and become involved in a small way in amalgamating resources and entering the arena of collective buying. The store executives also exchanged every kind of confidential statistical information and in this way were able to judge their own peformance against that of other similar operators. From time to time a group of senior executives from member stores would descend on one of the members and carry out a comprehensive "store study" lasting several days. On completion of this all-embracing scrutiny of the store's performance and organisation, a comprehensive report was produced in which complete frankness was exercised and no holds barred.

Such a study took place in Cambridge in 1973 - as we shall see in a later chapter - when those things which were lacking in the company were immediately recognised by the visiting professionals

One of those to join the firm after the war was Geoffrey Heath, the son of George Heath who had been in charge of four departments.

His war, as a second lieutenant with the 1st Bat., Gordon Highlanders had lasted just two months in action. Shrapnel, "from one side or the other" had smashed into his leg, confining him to hospital for a year and leaving him with a permanent limp.

He joined Eaden Lilley as a clerk with the intention of making a career for himself and like most other staff at that time saw the company as a lifetime employer.

"I had not been too sure what to do with my life before the war, but once I joined the company it quickly became obvious that it was the job for me," he says. And like other young men groomed for senior executive positions at the store he spent slightly over a year away from Cambridge learning the business. Both Kenneth and Howard Lilley, and later other members of the Lilley family, spent some time with other stores before returning to Cambridge.

Geoffrey Heath went to Grimwade Ridley at Oxford which was a food wholesale and retail business. His fiance worked in Reading and they sailed a boat on the river between the two towns.

Shortly after his return from Oxford he took over from his 80-year-old father the running of the retail and wholesale grocery department, the sundries department, and the paint department in the hardware section. By the early 1950s he had a staff of about 40 working for him plus the five travellers from the wholesale business. The working day started at 8.30am for the wholesale department, although the shop opened at 9.00am; all departments closed at 5.30pm. For those staff members who went home for lunch there was a one hour,15 minute break; for those that stayed at the store the break was only one hour. The store closed on Thursday afternoons, and the wholesale department closed on Saturdays, but as Geoffrey Heath looked after other sections he also worked all day Saturday.

Looking back Geoffrey Heath recalls that senior management was "extraordinarily relaxed" about the way departments were run, and the figures that were achieved.

"We were certainly not given financial targets; we simply did the best we could. It was extremely hard work, and we had a good idea of the day to day financial performance, but the overall results were organised on a company basis.

"If things were going wrong department heads were asked to explain, but usually there was little information available to us; we rather assumed that no news was good news.

"Questions about the amount of profit each department was producing per square foot, were just never asked," he says.

The late 1940s and early 1950s saw the start of a gradual reduction in the number of outside activities enjoyed by the 400 plus staff. For many years Eaden Lilley had its own rowing club, bowls club, tennis club, cricket club and football club, and ran an annual athletics event. In 1984 the Cambridge Evening News carried a series of photographs from the various clubs, which had been discovered in a bric-a-brac shop in the town. They showed the 1925-26 Lilley Football Club members, winners of the Cambridge and District Thursday League, and the Lilley Cricket Club, winners, in 1923, of the Thursday Division of the Cambridgeshire Junior League. The same batch of photographs produced a picture taken at the Grange Road rugby ground of about 400 people, "many of them in white sports gear and armed with tennis rackets. It looks like the firm's sports day."

Lilleys Boat Club - first boat - of 1938, with cox Don Murfet.

Minutes of meetings of various Lilley clubs have been kept over the years, including the the 1950 season of the Lilley Tennis Club where the captain was G.Mesney, the vice-captain Miss Spires, the secretary D.Cope and the treasurer Miss S.Wilks. By1958 the captain was M.Starns and secretary Miss E.Robinson, and the rules included "long sets shall not be played when other members are waiting to use the court" and "lost balls must be reported to the secretary."

Membership of the rowing club was restricted to employees, and in the mid 1930s it had great success in both "the bumps" and the "Time Race." The club continued until the start of the war when young men either volunteered or were called up. Survivors formed the 1947 Boat Club, but it fizzled out.

Kenneth Lilley was president of the boat club and vice-president of the Cambridgeshire Rowing Association.

The 1938 cox was Don Murfet, who, in 1985, was still working in the store's carpet department when the club was reformed and entered the City Bumps, under the instigation of Eaden Lilley's chef John Mansfield, who rowed with the University Sports Boat Club.

The annual outings continued for many years and were well supported by enthusiastic staff members. Shortly after the death of Walter Eaden Lilley some 350 employees sped off to Great Yarmouth on a specially chartered train, and then sat down to "an excellent luncheon" at Arnold's Restaurant. Kenneth Lilley made a short speech which concluded: "As the object of an outing is to be out I will not detain you any longer."

Many of the trips were organised by a sub committee from Lilley Amalgamated Clubs, whose members handed out the British Rail packed tea on the way back. They consisted, remembers one employee, of "a very tired looking roll, an apple and a piece of cake."

The "family" feeling was enhanced by clubs, outings and, of course the annual bonus, a Christmas party for the children of staff and Christmas gifts provided by the company. For many years all employees in the store received a chicken, the van drivers and warehousemen received beef and there were turkeys for the department heads. Storage and freezing problems encouraged a move to cash vouchers in later years.

Geoffrey Heath remembers as a boy the annual delivery of the turkey to his father on Christmas Eve. The van would arrive with an employee Harry Speed, who before working at Eaden Lilley had been a butcher, and his task was to dress the turkey for the lady of the house. He would disappear into the kitchen where he was provided with sherry and some mince pies, and within a short time had sorted out the turkey to its "oven ready" requirement. He would then move on to the next department head where he would repeat the work.

Despite the outer gloss of family unity there were some problems within the company, and certainly a strange attitude on importance of departments was developed in the 1950s. "I felt that the grocery and paint departments were, before a more egalitarian era, thought to be rather inferior by staff of other sections, particularly the furnishing departments," says Geoffrey Heath.

And the social standing of certain workers was also brought into doubt. Warehouse workers in the late 1940s and early 1950s were not allowed to go into the staff canteen, instead they had to bring sandwiches for lunch which were eaten in a coffee room in Green Street. The company employed a tea-lady on a part time basis to make tea and coffee for them at lunchtime.

"For some reason or other it was felt that the warehouse staff would be 'too rough' for the gentle employees of say the drapery department," says Geoffrey Heath, who fought and eventually won a battle to allow warehouse workers into the staff canteen.

Despite the sometime grievances there was never a call for a union branch to be formed at the company. When government legislation required the union options to be offered to workers a representative from USDAW visited the company and explained to staff the benefits of membership. Few staff joined.

"There were few negotiations with staff," says Geoffrey Heath. "There was an annual review of salary, plus the bonus, but if staff had not performed well they would not receive the bonus or a salary increase. I think that was taken as a fairly clear indication that they should look elsewhere for employment. Those that had done their job well, or made particular efforts during the year were given a one off payment, plus their bonus, plus a salary review.

"The management, however, was aware of salaries being paid to staff in other companies and a careful eye was kept to make sure that Eaden Lilley at least stayed in line with rival stores."

The annual review was a formal occasion.

Staff members lined up to be interviewed by a director, and an assessment of the employees' work and benefits to the company were detailed at the meeting. It was also an opportunity for staff members, if they dared, to detail any complaints or grumbles about the way they were treated or the work they were involved in, or even the relationship they had with their department head or buyer.

Progression, certainly in the 1950s, was largely through "dead man's shoes" although efforts were made to find promotion opportunities for particularly apt employees.

Geoffrey Heath, who went on to be the personnel manager, and was appointed to the board in 1974, launched a staff council in the mid 1980s.

The 1950s saw the arrival of many new staff including George Noble who, at the age of 15, had left the Central Grammar School for Boys and joined the company as an apprentice cabinet maker, in the workshops behind the furniture store at 38, Sidney Street. The workshops employed 24 staff involved in French polishing, cabinet making and reupholstery.

"My apprenticeship covered all aspects of furniture making and restoration," recalls George Noble, "together with being a 'journeyman' repairing furniture and fitting castors in customers' homes.

W. EADEN LILLEY & CO. LTD.   CAMBRIDGE

£120 Furnishing Scheme.

THE DINING ROOM.

Comfortable 3-Piece Suite comprising Settee and 2 Easy Chairs upholstered in Moquette of hard-wearing quality and luxuriously sprung, - - - - - -	£21 10 0
4 ft. Oak Sideboard of neat design with circular plate mirror in back, 2 cupboards and 2 drawers, - - - -	£7 19 6
Set of 1 Arm and 4 Small Dining Room Chairs with tip-out seats upholstered in Rexine, - - - - -	£8 2 6
Oak Dining Table of very solid construction, extending to 5 ft. × 3 ft., - - - - - - -	£5 15 0
Plate Mirror in Oak Frame, - - - - -	£1 15 0
9 ft. × 10 ft. 6 in. Seamless Pile Carpet, - - -	£5 15 6
Rug, - - - - - - - - -	£1 5 0
Oxydised Copper Curb, - - - - -	£0 19 6
Oxydised Copper Companion Set, - - - -	£0 12 9
	£53 14 9

Any Item can be Purchased Separately.

20

W. EADEN LILLEY & CO. LTD.   CAMBRIDGE

£120 Furnishing Scheme.

THE BEST BEDROOM.

Inlaid Mahogany Bedroom Suite of attractive design consisting of 4 ft. Wardrobe, fitted plate mirror in door, and long drawer underneath ; 3 ft. 6 in. Dressing Chest with swing mirror, 2 jewel boxes and 4 drawers ; 3 ft. Chest with boot cupboard and 2 long drawers, also 1 cane-seated Chair,	£26 17 6
Mahogany Bedstead to match Suite, supplied complete with wire mattress, wool mattress, feather bolster and 2 pillows,	£8 19 6
Bedroom Armchair covered in Cretonne, - - -	£2 10 0
10 ft. 6 ins. × 9 ft. Reversible Hair Carpet, - -	£4 12 6
Rug, - - - - - - - -	£0 12 6
Toilet Service, - - - - - - -	£1 5 6
Oxydised Copper Curb, - - - - -	£0 15 0
	£45 12 6

Any Item can be Purchased Separately.

21

The company reputation for "sound quality and workmanship" was emphasised in a special brochure dealing with home furnishings. Complete dining room and best bedroom schemes were offered at £120 each.

When he had completed his apprenticeship he was invited by Howard Lilley to take over shopfitting and maintenance of all company properties including staff houses.

"This involved the design and building of new shopfittings and resulted in the eventual refitting of all three floors of the Market Street store. To achieve this many long hours were worked, especially over weekends, which was against the ethos of the company," he says.

They were, however, assisted by Howard Lilley who offered to act as "chef" during the working on Saturday and Sunday nights, but his culinary skills were limited, mainly restricted to opening tins from the grocery department and heating them up in the company canteen.

George Noble's brother was a senior carpet fitter with the company, and his father had been a shop furniture porter.

"Eaden Lilley's was an institution, a band of people with a vast array of skills and high standards," he says.

But those skills had to be learned, and sometimes a lesson was taught the hard way. Junior sales assistant 15-year-old Pauline Impey had only been in the dress fabric department a few months when she was asked to iron some beautiful pink organza which had become creased in the window. She carefully carried the material upstairs to the dress department and set to with the iron; it took a while for her to discover that there was only one setting on the iron, and that was hot.

"With a face the same colour as the material I carried the organza back downstairs and showed the iron marks which covered the material," she recalls. Her department head, buyer Sydney Theobald was understanding, although he warned that it should never happen again.

She had joined the firm in the August of 1954 straight from school, and when, in 1999, Eaden Lilley closed its doors for the last time in Cambridge she had been the oldest continuous serving staff member.

In the 1950s there were 15 staff and two buyers in the dress fabric department. Later Sydney Theobald retired and was replaced by Kenneth Storey who came from a store in Nottingham.

For the first two or three months as a junior sales assistant Pauline Impey - later to become Pauline Rutterford when she married - was only allowed to watch the senior assistants as they sold goods. She was on hand to tidy up after any sales, and generally help out in the department.

Eventually the day came when she was allowed to serve her first customer, and the lady concerned wanted a brown worsted fabric. She was shown the range, and decided that it was not right.

"In those circumstances we had to refer the matter to a senior sales assistant in case she could help. My senior was Mrs Chard, who immediately showed the customer a brown worsted fabric, and much to my surprise the lady decided it was exactly the right material, and the sale was completed.

"I was surprised because I had already shown the customer that material, which had been rejected," says Pauline Rutterford.

The youngster was about to make the mistake of pointing out the detail when she felt the firm pressure of Mrs Chard's foot on her own shoe.

Life was very formal. When customers were around the assistants were all referred to by their surnames; they were not allowed to rush around the department, a proper pace was required. There was not a uniform although all assistants had to wear black, navy or dark grey.

"Before I started work my mother had bought some navy blue fabric from Eaden Lilley, which was made into a dress, together with two sets of white collars and cuffs, and that was my uniform for work."

Junior and senior assistants and many other employees cycled to work each day, and parked their cycles in a spot near the Green Street entrance - as did Kenneth Lilley who also cycled to work each day, and back again at lunchtime.

Pauline Rutterford has good memories of her lifetime at the store.

"The money was always pretty basic but the bonus helped and there was the kudos of working for such an important firm. I was pleased to start with them from school and was fairly sure from the very start that I wanted to stay with the company."

She was one of the first to attend a one-day a week release at the Cambridge Technical College to study for a City and Guilds retail certificate. The course covered maths, law and retail subjects. For a long while that was the only training available outside the firm.

After some 10 years she found herself with an opportunity to work for another firm, "but I decided to stay with Eaden Lilley. I am not sure whether that was loyalty to the firm or whether I just did not want to move on."

She became a senior assistant with Eaden Lilley, and stayed with the dress fabric department for 25 years until it was closed. She later moved to other departments including haberdashery and menswear, where they sold everything from pocket handkerchiefs to designer labelled suits.

For years, says Pauline Rutterford, assistants stayed behind their counters and waited for customers to approach them. In recent years they have switched to walking around the department and selling the products to customers and potential customers.

And the customers have also changed, but "we still try to give the same service, and I think Eaden Lilley has always had a good reputation for the attention it gives to customers."

Three years before Pauline Impey started work there was a visit to the store by Eileen Lilley, the wife of Howard, who had arrived to show staff her baby son, one -month-old William Eaden Lilley. It was his first view of the place that was to be his second home for many years, and although no one knew it at the time "Mr Eaden" was to oversee the biggest and most dramatic changes ever to take place at the store.

Memories
A family affair

Like all companies Eaden Lilley has had its fair share of staff turnover, but it has also had a remarkably high number of employees who have spent their working life with the store - and a goodly number who had relatives already working at the shop.

This chapter has already mentioned several family names that continue to crop up during the years, and is is no great surprise to find that generations of a family have worked in some capacity at the store.

From the management point of view there is a certain comfort factor in taking on the son or daughter of an employee; hard work and a good approach to the job are almost guaranteed, and any problems are likely to be sorted out by the family away from the gaze of employers.

From the family point of view the task is already well known in advance of employment. Sons, daughters, brothers and sisters, nieces and nephews step into a position that has at the very least been much discussed through the years, and is perhaps half understood before works starts. In the late 1800s and early 1900s it was accepted, and perhaps expected, that the children would follow in the footsteps of their parents, usually their father, subject to the right ability and attitude, and there being a vacancy.

As we have already seen the company itself has always encouraged a "family atmosphere" through a paternalistic attitude and a keen awareness of its staff and their abilities. There was a feeling by senior and middle management that everyone was working for the common good. It was often as easy for staff to ask advice from the employer as from parents. Youngsters entering service were encouraged to save, to look to a steady future, to be aware of the potential within the company, and maybe to understand their own limitations. In the mid 1950s where a senior director was also a director of the local building society, a good word was put in for young staff anxious to obtain their first mortgage. And the new house owners might easily find themselves playing host to Mr and Mrs Lilley or other members of the Lilley family who had arrived to see how they were settling in.

The chairman and senior directors took a regular, often daily, interest in each department and would walk through the store addressing each staff member by name, checking on the health of the family and providing words of encouragement and support.

The company heads - with the title of chairman or managing director - and members of the Lilley family, were always known by their first name, but referred to as Mr William, Mr Walter, Mr Kenneth or Mr Eaden, an unusual, old fashioned, but rather endearing term of address.

Being part of the Eaden Lilley "family" of workers is one of the points mentioned by every pensioner or former employee. Almost without exception they referred to the happy times, and the feeling that they were part of a team, able to involve themselves with the business and its development.

Arthur William Rutt, floorwalker and funeral director. (Cambridge Collection photograph)

It is possible to imagine that this management approach was developed, honed and expanded, but the most likely fact is that it was, and still is, a natural side of the Lilley family and that other senior managers fell in with the technique.

To a large extent it explains the emotional moments when it was announced that the store in Cambridge was to be closed. The tears and heartbreak were real reflections of the break-up of a family. As one employee explained: "I leave home to come to work, where I find I am at home again."

As you would expect lifelong involvement with the company was particularly strong in the earlier days of the company. There is evidence to support the theory that Logan Rutt, who was born in 1842 and was later employed as a draper's assistant, worked for Eaden Lilley; and there is the absolute fact that his son Arthur William Rutt spent his whole working life with the company. He was born in 1871, and started work with Eaden Lilley as soon as he was old enough. His marriage certificate of 1906, when he was 34, also describes his employment as a draper's assistant with his address as 14a, Market Hill, which looks like company accommodation or a hostel.

He, like many other lifelong staff members, progressed through the ranks, and by the time he retired in 1932 he was the firm's funeral director, an important and responsible post. At that time it was considered in Cambridge that "anyone who was anyone" had their funeral arrangements handled by Eaden Lilley, and the company was responsible for several society funerals involving an elaborate hearse drawn by horses properly dressed with black feathers.

Chapter 8

Are You Being Served?

T he "swinging sixties" burst upon an almost unsuspecting country bringing real changes in fashion, behaviour, language and attitudes - but life at W. Eaden Lilley & Co Ltd., continued at a more sedate pace.

The so-called "youth cult" and the dramatic influence of television was making an instant impact on the nation, and the number of married women in work rocketed, providing an extra income for the "affluent society."

Historian C.P.Hill writing in British Economic and Social History (1) says that apart from the rapid increase in car ownership there were several other indicators of British affluence in those years.

> *They included the vast multiplication of washing machines,refrigerators and power-driven gadgets of every sort; the spread of central heating; the extraordinary growth of foreign travel; a remarkable expansion in the range and style of ready-made clothing; the rise of the 'supermarket'; packaged and processed 'convenience' foods of every kind; the widespread increase in the custom of 'eating out'; and the emergence of the two-car family, often owning a cottage in the country as well as a suburban house. As the last example suggests, not all the changes were open to the majority of the population. But most were, in varying measures, thanks to the great rise in personal incomes during these years.*

Education, improvement in the health service and a variety of social reforms were an added bonus from the development of the affluent society.

Although perhaps not keeping pace with the changes of style in London, the Cambridge store was also looking to the younger, relatively wealthy customers, and had modernised its operations to meet the new demand.

A feature in the quality magazine East Anglia Life in September, 1964 referred to the "modern business" and the "huge up-to-the-minute store." It enthused about the various departments including the "vast gown showroom"; soft furnishings and carpets which offered "a wide variety of qualities and colourings to satisfy the tastes of young and old alike," and the "impressive stock of modern and traditional furniture" which included Scandinavian design, all the rage in the 1960s.

But like the best of the television series "Are you being served" what the customer saw at the front was not always what was happening behind the scenes.

Perhaps in the spirit of the day, which encouraged freedom of speech and a more outspoken approach to the workplace an avant garde magazine sprung up within the company, initially produced by the staff without management backing, but later with more direct involvement from senior executives.

Its joint editors S.Robertson and R.Keeley, freely admitted that it was not the most popular publication every produced, and recorded that some members of the 500 staff were seen to tear it up when it was delivered to their departments. It contained a rather strange mix of department news, reviews of shows, films and records, discussions on Christianity and a variety of other matters including some irreverent glances at departments and their employees. It also appeared to reflect some of the tougher views of staff.

Dealing with the lot of the shop assistant - "which is not a happy one" - in November 1963, the magazine, titled AIM, the Sports and Social Club staff magazine, said assistants must have a great deal more patience than factory workers, that wage scales "are dismally inadequate compared with industry" and that the five day week was no nearer introduction, "although a number of retailers in the town have proved that it can work if given the opportunity.

"The procrastination concerning this latter point is something which most shop assistants have tolerated passively for a very long time, but they have a right to know that the promise made over a year ago by the Chamber of Trade that something will be done, has not been forgotten or once more pushed to the back of the shelf and allowed to moulder."

An earlier issue had roundly condemned "the one commodity that is never in short supply at W Eaden Lilley & Co.," and remained unaffected by seasonal fluctuations - gossip.

Editor R.Keeley said that the gossip was "slanderous, malicious backbiting, which travels by a nauseous route known as the 'Lilley Grapevine' and from which few of us seem to be exempt." More than a page was given over to the subject.

Later larger issues of AIM were more in line with other staff magazines, but by the mid 1960s the back page carried a drawing of a coffin with "Lilies for remembrance" and a note explaining: "Due to general apathy and lack of contributions the editor regrets AIM has become AIMLESS."

Among those to join the company early in the decade was 28-year-old Jill Coutts who had previously worked in a chemist shop in the town which had been forced to close. A Max Factor representative knew she was looking for a job and introduced her to the company where she was interviewed by Geoffrey Heath, before starting in 1962 as an assistant in the perfumery and toiletry and cosmetics department. For the first six months she " hardly saw daylight" working in the stockroom unpacking, checking and putting stock away, which gave her a firm background knowledge of the stock available.

"The one thing I did hate was wearing the white linen overall with buttons all down the front, which was required in the department. It somehow made you feel inferior to the rest of the staff."

The perfumery section was a small part of the department with the majority given over to everyday toiletries.

After a while she left to have a daughter, and returned three months later, but this time to fill a vacancy in the china and glass department."I was a little cautious at first because it was a new department to me, but I quickly grew to love it and had a wonderful time there." The department was moved six times over the years.

The formality of the store remained even in the late 1960s and early 1970s. "The fashion department always gave the impression that they were the cream of the crop; the buyer always wore a hat and the fashion staff were allowed to wear their own clothes, rather than a uniform. They were also at the top of the store, and there was a tendency to look down on other departments."

Strict rules still remained at coffee and lunch breaks with men and women segregated, and separate facilities for buyers and directors. It was, says Jill Coutts, an exact parallel to "Are you being Served."

But despite the slightly stilted atmosphere there was still a great family feeling within the firm.

"The directors would tour the store every day saying 'good morning' to the staff. They always seemed to know if we had been on holiday, if it was a birthday or even if there had been a death in the family."

Within a few years an opportunity arose for her to take over as buyer for the china and glassware department. She was, at first, concerned with the paperwork involved, but after conversations with other buyers, including explanations on how to read and understand a computer sheet, she accepted the job, and stayed in that position until the change overs caused by the restructuring in the 1980s.

The 1960s saw some substantial changes in the physical appearance of the store, including a two year long rebuilding scheme. The decision to close the wholesale grocery business from "such a limited central site" meant that the space and capital released could be used to develop retail activities; a similar decision was made on the wholesale drapery department. In both cases the majority of staff were transferred to other departments. The vacant area, plus the space earned by acquiring Smarts the Tailor at 11, Market Street, was then rebuilt and added to the side and rear of the main store. Work started in 1967 and ended in 1969, and, said an internal report at the time: "The need to maintain 'business as usual' made this a long and, on occasions, a wet and dusty business."

At about the same time Trinity College, landlords of the Sidney Street property used by Eaden Lilley to house the furniture department since 1896, decided to rebuild on the site. That involved moving the department to the main store. The move started in September, 1968 shortly before demolition was due, and was heavily complicated by traffic conditions in the town centre which required that the work was carried out on Sundays during the month. More than 12,000 sq ft of furniture was moved in three weekends.

Howard Lilley said at the time: "It worked much more smoothly than expected. This was partly because stocks were intentionally run down for a while, and we delayed deliveries until after the move."

The Sidney Street showrooms had become difficult for customers who had to work their way around five floors to view the furniture selection. After the move most of the display was on the first floor of the main Market Street building. The Cambridge Evening News said in October that year that "one of the most distinctive features is the furniture department's unusual ceiling, midnight blue. This is studied with small spotlights and provides an effective foil for the attractive displays there."

It said lovers of fine quality reproduction work "have long brought their custom to Eaden Lilley. They will still find the beautiful mahogany pieces of Regency times and the ever-popular oak dining suits and dressers which are ideal for cottage or mansion." And, presumably in an effort to appeal to its younger readers, the newspaper added there was plenty to attract them including "way out" shining white fibreglass dining suites and the latest range of linked furniture for bedrooms.

The one time non-conformist chapel in the Market Street building had been converted for the sale of office furniture, armchairs, coffee tables and other items. The room had started life as a Congregationalists meeting room, was used from 1929 as a Weslyan Chapel, then by the famous Cambridge Union Society as a debating chamber and finally as a billiard saloon before being acquired by the firm in 1920.

The 1960s make-over of the store also brought improvements and changes to other departments including the bedding department which now had an entrance through the fabric section on the ground floor, and another leading from the back of the furniture department on the first floor. It offered a wide variety of beds and mattresses including those for customers suffering from back complaints. It also sold "his" and 'hers" pillows which provided varying degrees of firmness.

The bedding department was the only one to have stayed in the same place for more than 80 years. By 1970, all but three departments had been completely moved at least once, and in several cases two or three times.

The wholesale grocery and drapery departments, closed to make way for expansion, had produced a great deal of work for the general office of Eaden Lilley which was responsible for sending out all the invoices from the departments at the back of the main store. The staff there were joined by young Terry Langley in November, 1957; his father knew one of the buyers who had organised an interview for the youngster who had only been out of school for six months. Initial work included casting up the invoices which were then sent to the typing pool. His starting salary was £3-8/7d.

Two years later he was asked to move to the cashier's office on the ground floor. The offices were under the direct charge of company secretary R. B. Horne.

The stairs and lifts were part of life at Eaden Lilley for many years. The lifts had inter-connecting doors enabling passengers to walk through from one to the other should there be a breakdown.

A unique Caithness Glass goblet, which contains an 1890 half crown, was presented by Barclays Bank to W.Eaden Lilley & Co., to mark 100 years of association between the two companies.

Early duties in the cashier's office included cashing up and handling customer accounts, with the difference that in the 1960s nearly every transaction was in cash. If, on a rare occasion, a customer payment was made by cheque someone from the department would bring it to the cashier's office where it was exchanged for cash and then put through the till.

The office ran on a staff of four including the chief cashier. Dress code insisted on a white shirt and a suit, with the jacket remaining on throughout the hottest weather.

Fountain pens, not biros, had to be used at all times, and as was the custom at that time, each receipt for monies received had to include a postage stamp. Wages, issued from the wages office next door, were always in cash in small brown envelopes.

"Cash collections were carried out from every department during the afternoons. It was all taken back to the office and later to the night safe of one of the local banks," says Terry Langley. Substantial sums of cash, often running into thousands of pounds, were taken from the store to the bank each day. Later security measures dictated that a cashier should be accompanied by at least two other staff on his trip to Barclays, and by the mid 1970s security firms were used to collect cash, following the mugging of two employees from another company.

Bringing change into the store was another problem and three cashiers were needed to collect the bags of coins from the bank.

In 1990 a special lunch was held to mark the centenary of the connection between W.Eaden Lilley & Co., and Barclays Bank, known in the 1890s as Mortlocks. A special brochure produced for the event showed several highlights of the 100 years including the £22,000 advance from the bank in 1920 which enabled the purchase of Market Street and Green Street freeholds from the University Financial Board.

The colourful advertising executive at the time, Marion Read, who had a well known talent for verse, penned some lines for the opening pages of the brochure which included:-

> *Did our accountant - learned gent*
> *Over dusty ledgers bent*
> *Perched on high stool, late at night*
> *Counting farthings by gas light*
> *Pause awhile to dream and ponder*
> *On these present times we wonder?*
> *No doubt he would have felt surprise*
> *To see this thriving enterprise*
> *A hundred years ahead from when*
> *He totted columns with quill pen -*
> *Now passed via automatic tills*
> *From earlier coins and entry bills*
> *To electronic transfer - and*
> *The money rarely touched by hand.*

Cheques universally replaced cash in the progress of financial affairs, and by the 1990s credit and debit cards swept on to the scene. Last year (1999) fewer than 20 cheques a day were being presented at the store.

Unlike some stores the change over to credit cards was quickly taken on board by the firm, even though credit card slips had to be made out manually and details listed in the cashier's office. The subsequent change to swipe cards cut down the workload throughout the store, with totals listed by the tills at the end of each day.

The wages office on the ground floor had been the first working home for Robert Horne, whose father had been a director at Eaden Lilley, and who joined the firm in 1950, aged 24, after studying as an articled clerk. His studies were interrupted by two-and-a-half years war service in the Royal Navy, largely in the Far east.

There was little mechanisation, and up to 400 people to provide with cash wages every week. A series of cards were used to detail payments, minus tax, pension payments and other items. Each packet had to be made up manually and was put into boxes for delivery to different departments, and then handed out by the floor walkers. There were no pay chits with the money; it was assumed each staff member would know his own wages.

Robert Horne still recalls some salaries in the 1950s, a van driver earned about £3-00 a week, his mate about £2-10/- a week, out of which they paid 3/- towards their pension and a small amount in National Insurance.

Overtime payments were particularly high during the May Ball season in Cambridge, as Eaden Lilley provided marquees, furniture and fittings, and even a portable dance floor. For the 20 women in the workrooms at the back of the store there was a big demand for the fittings, and staff were required to work all day erecting the marquee, and then had to be on tap overnight to take it down and move to another college for the next ball. The firm was used for about 80 per cent of the balls in Cambridge.

"The pace of life was different in those days," says Robert Horne. "The floorwalkers would escort customers from one department to another; there was a real concern to see that everybody was happy with the goods they had bought, and alterations to dresses and suits were carried out as quickly as possible. On the fashion floor customers were simply not allowed to leave if the dress did not fit perfectly."

As least two of the floorwalkers had a secret life; they doubled as undertakers when the funeral department became busy.

Within a couple of years Robert Horne had moved to the accounts department looking after quarterly, monthly and overdue accounts. At the same time his father was still working at the store, and stayed there until he retired in 1969.

"It really was like one great big family in those days; we were small enough for everybody to know each other and we all seemed to get along very well. We worked hard, five a half days a week, but there were plenty of things to do in the evenings, dances, the cinema, whist drives and sports club, together with a trip to London at least once a month."

First job for the office staff each morning was to open the post. All mail was delivered to the main Market Street store and then hand delivered by Kenneth Lilley, Howard Lilley and Cyril Mack to other departments around the town. Large quantities of post included orders, payments and requests for help and information.

Robert Horne's wife-to-be Betty started work at Eaden Lilley straight from school in 1954, working under George Heath in the sale of wholesale and retail soaps and cosmetics.

She had only been there a week when George Heath insisted that she learn the three codes used in the department - retail, wholesale and cost. "I had to memorise the lists within a week. I did it then, and I can still remember them now," she says.

George Heath, by then an old man and shortly to retire, terrified 15-year-old Betty and several other staff members in the departments he controlled. When his son Geoffrey took over there was a sudden change in the atmosphere.

Over the next couple of years Betty and Robert saw each other at work from time to time, and later met at a tea-dance in the town. They were engaged and married when Betty was 21. The wedding was attended by Kenneth Lilley and other directors - and held on a Thursday afternoon. It was certainly not unusual for couples who had met at work to marry when finances permitted, and after the war there was no requirement to ask for board approval.

Sale time, held twice a year, was well attended and usually started with a queue of between 150 and 200 customers waiting outside the main store for the 9.00am deadline. "They were real bargains at that time, existing stock which had been reduced, rather than items bought in especially for the sale," says Robert Horne. Bargains in the bedding department were particularly sought.

Then the sweeping staircase and central well were still in place; the well eventually being filled in during 1959.

Kenneth Eaden Lilley, pictured in the 1980s

Betty Horne went back to the store eight years after her marriage, but this time working in a newly introduced concession fashion department.

Robert Horne stayed in the accounts department until he retired and saw a variety of changes including the introduction and development of computerisation.

Some physical changes made during the early 1970s to the store included reducing by half the shop front, built in 1930, and providing staff restaurant and rest rooms on the second floor. The firm was also troubled by the future of 23,Market Street, opposite the main store entrance, which housed the carpets and soft furnishings departments, and was leased from Cambridge Corporation and the Trustees of Henry Martyn Hall.

"The design of the building has major disadvantages and we have been unable to obtain permission to increase the floor area, except on the ground floor. We believe that the direct entrance into the departments from the street does much to outweigh the unfavourable conditions under which these sections operate; the window space has been particularly valuable since the shop front of the main store was reduced," said a report compiled in 1973.

It also produced some figures which showed total retail sales including grocery reached £1,857,000 in 1970-71; increased to £2.072,000 in 1971-72 and £2,520,000 in 1972-73. The directors were listed as chairman Kenneth Lilley, Howard Lilley in charge of merchandise, shop fitting and display, Cyril Mack in charge of merchandise furnishing and transport, and F.C.J.Webb, company secretary and accountant who also looked after the office. The intermediate management consisted of executive manager G.J.Heath, store manager H.E.Gigney and merchandise controller A.MacManus.

At the time the company employed 418 staff made up of 41 full time buyers-managers; 150 full time and 54 part time selling staff; 32 full time and 17 part time accounts and clerical; 42 full time and eight part time workrooms and workshops; six in advertising and display; 19 full and part time in maintenance and cleaning; 11 in transport; 12 in full and part time catering and 22 full and part time in warehouse work.

(1) British Economic and Social History, 1700-1982, by C.P.Hill; published by Edward Arnold Publishing, 1985.

Mr Kirkup's happy kindergarten

Sid Kirkup was not pleased about the prospect of running the toys, games and baby-carriages department at Eaden Lilley. The directors had promised that it would be an easy time for him in the department after its previous head had retired.

But Sid knew better. "There was no easy bit in any department", he said later.

Wisely he did not reflect these views to his staff, who were more than keen to work in "Mr Kirkup's happy kindergarten," in the mid 1950s.

His smiling band included Pat Wilson, Elaine Ellum, Irene Harrison, Peggy Matthews and Adie Kent - formerly Rabbitt.

Adie joined the team in the autumn of 1956 ready for the pre-Christmas rush.

"We were in the basement - they call it the lower ground floor these days. A lift was used to visit the department and the floor walker Mr Mumford was often on hand to open the doors.

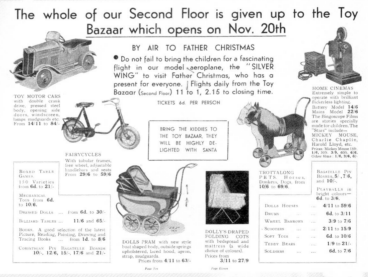

Christmas in the toy department included toy motor cars, dollshouses, prams, "fairycylces" home cinema, Mickey Mouse and a chance to visit Father Christmas on the silver wing model aircraft.

"The walls were all lined with mahogany and glass cases. An alley-way led to the packing department where the most unlikely shapes were wrapped with great expertise and speed."

She said that Mr Kirkup ruled his department with "humour, intelligence and goodwill, and Mr Mumford had no cause to worry about us.

"We were all in charge of our own sections, and Mr Kirkup's deputy Maurice Barber was responsible for all technical jobs, fixing and assembling anything with wheels, and for providing technical information for customers."

The baby-carriages were the best in the business with large well sprung wheels, and extra equipment that included storm windows, sun shades and cat nets. When the youngsters started walking Miss Ellum sold their parents reins with bells, in cream, pink and blue.

Row upon row of metal or lead soldiers were displayed by Mrs Matthews, "whose days in the WAAFS gave her a taste for creating artistic battlefields," says Adie. She also sold Matchbox and Dinky toys.

Mrs Dobson and Mrs Brenda Oakman kept the pens, stationery, birthday cards and games section. Mrs Irene Harrison, assisted by Adie, ordered books, dolls and soft toys. They included teddy bears produced by firms like Chiltern, Chad Valley and Pedigree and which have since become collectors items.

And there were dolls in white, black and brown.

Books included the Ladybird selection, Enid Blyton's "Famous Five" and classic fairy-tales which "simply flew off the shelves at Christmas."

There was a regular parade of the famous and not-so-famous TV and theatre stars who came to buy in the children's department, including Eleanor Bron who confessed to "having a thing about elephants" and bought a great grey toy with all the Beyond the Fringe cast in attendance.

The department success for Sid Kirkup came towards the end of a 50-year plus career with Eaden Lilley. He joined the company in 1917, and worked as a stock keeper in the brass cellar, and he was also responsible for mats and matting, including hemp carpets 18in to 36in wide, and coconut matting in widths up to 72in.

In notes he provided for the company after his retirement in 1969 he said that in the early days everything had to stand off the floor because storms would flood the basement to a depth of two to three inches.

They were not required to "clock-in" in the early days, but a senior employee, Fred Gates, would keep a note if anyone was late and it would be passed on to the directors "to be taken into account at bonus time."

The Cambridge May week ball was a busy time for Sid and his department, as they had to provide all the carpets and red felt used for supper tents, together with hair brushes and combs for the ladies cloak room and powder from another department. Hundreds of fairy lights were also provided by Eaden Lilley under the watchful eye of Charles Rutt who would make sure that faulty bulbs were replaced as quickly as possible.

"The managing director at this time was Mr Walter Lilley who was also a director of the local building society. He used to advise us young lads to take out a share in the society, and that was used as a deposit for our first house.

"Harry Fitch was 'front man' for the department. He came out of retirement during the First World War. He was rather a gruff man, but I got on well enough with him."

Years later he took over the toy and pram department. "I was rather pushed into it, and I was not too happy about it at the time, but I enjoyed it later."

To those who mentioned that his life may have been a little "hum-drum" Sid Kirkup used to say that a great amount of trust went into the job "and I enjoyed the directors' confidence."

Chapter 9

"Energy, willingness, interest, ability"

Life on the shop floor at Eaden Lilley & Co Ltd continued at a comfortable pace during the 1970s and 1980s, although top management did not always agree about the way forward.

Whilst Howard Lilley and the other relatively newly appointed directors recognised the urgent need to move with the times, the chairman's natural caution in all things was frequently the cause of irritation and frustration on the part of his colleagues. He was not a natural merchant and preferred to devote his time and energies to those aspects of running the business which interested him most. An engineer at heart, these tended to centre around mechanical things rather than merchandise issues. To his great credit he was also a very caring person and was concerned always for the welfare of everyone who worked in the company.

Howard Lilley, pictured in the 1980s

As well as being entirely admirable this also had its down side and resulted in a serious reluctance to let people go, either by virtue of under-performance or by reason of age. The inevitable result was that there were some passengers on board and the average age of staff was too high. Sadly the chairman insisted on retaining ultimate authority and decision-making was frequently an extremely laborious process involving much procrastination.

In the early 1970s the firm, like thousands of others, struggled through a succession of industrial disputes, strikes and pay demands. It started with the postal workers in 1971, followed by the miners and then the power workers and railwaymen. A three day week was declared, power cuts were introduced and shops were only allowed to use electricity on the days allocated to them by electricity boards. Non-power days meant providing lamps or candles to light the shops and stores around the country.

To add to problems there was a worldwide shortage of petrol because of the Arab-Israeli war, a 50mph speed limited was introduced and petrol ration books issued.

On top of that the store executives felt they were getting a rough deal from traffic congestion in the city, and an experimental one-way system which was thought to be detrimental to trade.

They did, however, have a good idea of where their customers were coming from, largely the city, university and surrounding district up to a radius of some 40 miles, according to an internal report. Population, at about 100,000, was not expanding and employment depended to a large extent directly or indirectly on the university.

Enormous efforts were made, in the autumn of 1973, in anticipation of a store study for and by members of the Independent Stores Association (ISA). Executives from other stores descended on Eaden Lilley departments and commented on what improvements or changes should be made, a move that must have created some interesting response from the store's buyers-managers when they met for a quiet drink after work.

One visiting director took a look at affairs within the personnel management and staff training side of the company, a department run by Geoffrey Heath with Miss A.M. Heckford as staff trainer. He found that staff relations were generally excellent, and had the impression that it was a happy store.

"There is little formal organisation," he said, "and a great deal of loyalty and sympathetic understanding between management, buyers and all staff. The family store atmosphere has successfully overcome the problems of staffing in an area of one per cent unemployment and the consequent highly competitive demand for staff. The premises are old, and these do cause the problems of difficult working conditions, but the staff accept them."

On staff conditions he said there was an employee's discount of 15 per cent for all staff irrespective of status. The staff restaurant and lounge were being improved, sick pay entitlements were normal and frequently exceeded in individual cases after consideration by the directors, and holiday entitlements were three weeks generally and four weeks for buyers. The pension scheme was being revised to improve the benefits.

He said there was not a staff committee or any other body to represent the views of the staff in general, but that the excellent relations between the directors, management and staff have made "for good verbal interchange at all levels and the need for formal bulletins and notices has been unnecessary."

Generally the ISA members seemed pretty impressed with what they found but complained of cramped conditions and an old fashioned approach to several departments. Interestingly the report on the executive organisation was "sent separately" and not included in the pack available at the time. What is known, however, is that it contained a strong recommendation that a professional merchandise executive should be brought in from outside, but it took the best part of another five years before they eventually recruited Michael Marriott from a fellow member of ISA in Yorkshire, which had been taken over by House of Fraser the previous year. Somebody was badly needed to inject new life into this wonderful business, already 225 years old. Michael Marriott happened to appear on the scene at the right moment and exactly filled the role of catalyst.

The store study also cited lack of space and clutter in several of its reports including one on the furniture department, which was "approached through a maze of coat stands", and dresses and suits, "hemmed in by the encroachment of the separates department," and coats and raincoats, "very tight and congested area."

One ISA member found the warehousing workrooms in Mill Lane "fascinating as customer's re-upholstery, mattress remaking and cabinet work is carried on in a very traditional manner. I particularly liked the stock of suede and was honoured to see Randolph Churchill's chair."

Michael Marriott was recruited from an ISA store in Yorkshire.

Entering Jack Cox's menswear department the ISA man felt he was entering "a small, rather old-fashioned, independent shop. There is little to suggest that it is part of the store." He said there were 53 mens outfitters in Cambridge, including "boutiques, the multiples, half dead traditional shops and a few excellent competitors - Austin Reed, Hornes and Joshua Taylor." He said that Jack Cox should "be more venturesome, go for more colour in his ranges and try the higher priced lines even if this initially means a lower stockturn.

"Menswear is still a growth trade and at the moment Mr Cox has only three top competitors that need to worry him."

Dealing with the corsetry and underwear department another ISA man said it should be moved away from the top of the stairs and a little off the main thoroughfare.

One ISA man found the soft furnishing department including the workroom tidy and clean and the staff "cheerful and efficient" under buyer manager Bob Josh.

He had served a three year apprenticeship at Knight and Gealer a small furniture shop in Reigate, before moving to the soft furnishing department of Shinners' of Sutton, earning £2 a week plus 1.5d commission on every item he sold. The war years saw him at 20 serving with the Royal Air Force as a ground gunner, a unit later developed into the famous RAF Regiment. Posted to the Far East he later volunteered for parachute training despite only being married for six months. The objective of 2810 Squadron of the RAF Regiment was to be parachuted behind enemy lines in Burma and set up visual control point(VCPs), and with the use of radio help direct fire on to enemy targets. Bob Josh made one drop behind the lines before the war ended.

On his return to the store in Sutton he was advised to ask for £6 a week, which he received. A colleague at the store who was too old for war service was still on £3 a week, but had made substantial commission during the war by the sale of "black-out" material.

He later moved to become a representative earning "the magical figure of £500 a year." Saturdays and Sundays were spent ironing the samples ready for show during the forthcoming week. During his travels he visited Eaden Lilley and got to know the buyer Cyril Mack, nephew of the former managing director of the company. A short time later he applied for a job with the Cambridge store and after being interviewed by Kenneth Lilley, started as a salesman in soft furnishing. The company removal department helped him move from Wimbledon to a top flat in Selwyn Gardens in Cambridge, the bottom flat being occupied by a secretary at the store and the middle flat by Miss Spiers, buyer in the children's department.

In the 1950s the department was based in the Henry Martyn Hall, and within days Bob Josh was at work. "You could certainly tell in those days if the customer had money. We would look at the way a woman was dressed, if she had a crocodile handbag and crocodile shoes, or in the winter a fur coat, we knew there was money about.

"But I never attempted to sell a 4/11d cloth to a woman I knew could really only pay 2/11d."

After years of experience in the business he was also able to spot the professions of customers with uncanny skill. "I could tell the difference between say a teacher and a civil servant. They had a different approach to life, and with a little bit of studying I had a very good idea of the customer's life."

A while after his arrival at the store Cyril Mack was promoted to a directorship and another employee promoted to buyer. Bob Josh decided that it was not a situation he could accept, and applied for another job in Luton which was offered to him. He saw Cyril Mack to ask for a meeting with Kenneth Lilley because he wanted to hand in his notice . The director told him: "Go? You can't possibly go. We will do something for you, don't you worry."

"I was impressed, but in Cambridge, especially after Sutton, everything moved at a snail's pace. Eventually he came along and said that it had been decided that the other man, a Mr Gray, would buy linen, weaves and other material, and I would be responsible for silk damask. I explained that two buyers in the same smallish department could not possibly work." Bob Josh rejected the proposal, but agreed to stay with an increased salary and the privileges of a buyer, including use of the buyer's dining room which offered waitress service. He effectively became a "silent buyer" and when Mr Gray retired he took over as full time buyer, a job he held for nearly 20 years until he retired in 1985.

And as a buyer he was looking for certain qualities in the materials presented to him by reps. First on the list was colour, followed by quality of colour, including tone of colour, and then the excellence of the cloth.

Any rep who was not able to detail the exact content of material without referring to his book was unlikely to receive the business from Bob Josh.

Back in the 1970s the Independent Stores Association had, by the middle of the decade, merged with Associated Department Stores (ADS), to provide "buying muscle to rival any of the major publicly quoted groups." The new organisation, known as Associated Independent Stores (AIS) was a retailer-owned co-operative group of around 100 small to medium sized independent stores with roots going back to the formation of the British Merchandising Club in 1927. As well as Eaden Lilley members included Bentalls in the south of England, Beales of Bournemouth, Elys of Wimbledon and Joplings of Sunderland.

AIS was to start with a joint turnover of around £200m, which rivalled most of the big publicly quoted groups and represented some 20 per cent of total store turnover in the country. The AIS was to provide a lifeline to the small independent stores who found themselves up against tough competition from department stores like House of Fraser, the John Lewis Partnership and Debenhams, stores which had been steadily increasing market share from the early 1950s.

An article by Elinor Goodman in The Financial Times in October, 1975 said ADS members were buying about 35 per cent of their merchandise through the central buying organisation with penetration as high as 60 per cent in some fields.

Traditionally the two associations have tended to be somewhat jealous of each other's activities and regarded their own approach to co-operation as the right one - hence the two previous attempts to merge which failed. But now there seems to be the will to make a go of it. George Walton, acting as an informal advisor to the two associations, seems to have convinced the two boards that only by such co-operation will they be able to achieve anything like the success of either the Dutch group Hobo-Faam or Katag.

The decade also brought new efforts to deal with the problem of staffing levels and the personnel department produced a message to school leavers which promised a "great variety of employment" at the store, and offered good working conditions and training. The firm provided details of careers available in retailing including selling, buying, management, clerical, window dressing, advertising, stock keeping, accountancy, maintenance, warehousing, dispatch, workrooms and catering. It said there were 160 salespeople selling at the store, and another 220 behind the scenes. It provided in-store training and outside store training by day release courses and home study courses. The store took entrants with all levels of education standards from almost no qualifications through to those with degrees.

"Though qualifications are important, as important, or more important, are the right qualities.

"We look for:-

1) Personality - ability to take to and get on with people - explain things, sympathy.

2) Energy - willingness, interest, ability.

3) Appearance - smartly dressed - well groomed.

4) Ability to write and speak good, clear English.

5) Good manners and common sense.

6) Ability in maths.

7) Practical and artistic ability."

It said wages were £1,404 at 16-years-old and £2002 at 21-years-old.

In line with changes around the country the store was opening in the 1970s from 9.00am to 5-30pm between Tuesday and Saturday, with late night shopping on Wednesday until 7-30pm. It was closed all day on Mondays, except in December.

Apart from the new staff restaurant and rest rooms, there were few major changes in the buildings during the 1970s, but that did not stop an almost constant shift in departments and sections as management looked to provide better placings for the 29 departments, the counters and staff.

One of those involved in the day to day change-around was Graham Livermore who had joined Eaden Lilley in 1970, starting in the cabinet shop in Mill Lane. The apprenticeship scheme had been scrapped a few years earlier but as a 16-year-old trainee he was taught the finer points of furniture repairs, renovations and woodwork. He was also reminded of the role of a trainee which required plenty of sweeping up, tea making and, every now and again, unloading coffins which were delivered to the funeral parlour, also in Mill Lane. The cabinet shop was, he says, remarkably old fashioned for the 1970s, but it meant that he learned his trade the "old fashioned way" which stood him in good stead in the years ahead.

Some of the work meant travelling to customers' homes - flat pack wardrobes, for example, were erected by Eaden Lilley staff once they had been sold - and also to the colleges in Cambridge particularly during the holiday period when broken furniture and equipment had to be repaired.

Every Monday he spent a day with the shopfitting team at the store and eventually was moved full time into that department, which had three shopfitters plus an electrician.

The decision to move a department involved a considerable amount of effort for department staffers and the shopfitting team. It took anything up to three weeks for the shopfitting manager and his team to organise the move and prepare the operation for the change-over which always had to take place when the store was closed over the weekend. Shelves, counters, plug points, display racks and much more had to be slotted into place or erected in time for the Monday morning opening.

"It was," says Graham Livermore, "absolute mad panic, but great fun."

By the early 1990s shopfitting had been switched to an outside firm. Graham Livermore stayed with the company looking after a variety of maintenance and other requirements.

At about the same time the store was struck by a flood which caused thousands of pounds worth of damage. The flood started sometime during the evening of Maundy Thursday in 1991 when the store was closed. Contractors had been working on a 6in mains pipe in the store's basement, and had sealed the pipe before leaving for the Easter break. The protective sleeve over the pipe burst and within minutes water was pouring into the basement.

The fire brigade took until Good Friday evening to pump out all the water by which time the firm's electrician and Graham Livermore had managed to retrieve and dry off some of the main fuseboard switches in a company oven.

Michael Marriott, then managing director of the firm told local newspapers: "It is mayhem down there, total chaos. There is no way we can say how long it will take to dry it out, but we are talking about a matter of weeks."

About 30 volunteer staff arrived at the store to help pile the damaged goods into vans to be taken to warehouses.

In fact it took just 13 days before the basement was reopened, and staff had worked for more than 4,000 hours to mop and repair the damaged area. The refit cost £100,000. Stocks were replenished, a new floor covering laid down and the entire area redecorated.

"It was carried out in record time and was an object lesson in teamwork," said Michael Marriott.

All these problems were still a long way ahead for the future managing director Eaden Lilley who had been introduced to the staff at less than one month old. As a toddler there were trips with his mother Eileen to the lingerie department where he was left in the charge of a shop assistant while his mother tried on the latest fashions. He spent the time playing with the black price tickets.

His mother had been through a difficult time with the death of her first husband Neil Whitley who had been a surgeon with the Black Watch. He was badly injured parachuting into Europe on D-Day, and died later from his injuries. They had a son, Michael.

The best man at their wedding had been Howard Lilley who later married Eileen, who had been a nurse during the war. June, 1951 saw the arrival of William Eaden Lilley - always known as Eaden - on the scene, and his introduction to the store and a goodly portion of its 400 employees. The boy and his step-brother, who suffered from polio, were regular visitors to the Market Street premises.

"My very early memories of the store are a little vague, but they are helped by photographs of the firm taken at the time. I certainly remember areas like the well, which was taken out in 1959, and the main staircase, together with the wrought iron gates of the lifts. Everything was mahogany, with a terrific gloss to the wooden counters."

Glorious trips to the store at Christmas also figure in the memories of Eaden Lilley, with Father Christmas, the grotto, and a theme linked to the Cambridge Arts Theatre pantomime.

"The store is those days was not so compact, it was more spread out. There seemed to be a lot more space, and departments like the fashion section seemed enormous."

Even at an early age he was aware that he was the son of the deputy chairman, and knew that he was being treated in a different way to other customers. He certainly remembers at Christmas going to the wholesale buyer Arthur Newman, and being offered a selection of gifts for his mother. One year he ordered a tapestry cushion, which in 1999 was still in the family.

His early education was in Cambridge, including some time at St Faith's School, before moving to a boarding school just outside Norwich. Having the same name as the department store there were some small problems at school, but he does not recall they were a particular difficulty. In later years, however, the name did cause confusion. Cycling to work in the 1990s he fell off the bicycle and broke a wrist. An ambulance was called and one of the early questions was "What is your name?"

"Eaden Lilley," he replied.

The ambulance driver clearly thought his patient was suffering from concussion because he carefully explained: "No, that is where you work - what is your name?"

Back at school his GCE results left a little to be desired and so he returned to a college in Cambridge for more studies. He finished up with five "O" levels and then moved on to a business studies course.

He was, at that stage, still uncertain of his career path. There was, of course, every opportunity to join the family business, but he was very tempted by farming, possibly because his grandparents had owned the model farm at Grantchester.

He had been working on Saturdays at the store, usually in the menswear and boyswear departments, and although his parents never exerted any pressure on him to join the business, he eventually decided that he would like to be involved with the firm.

In line with family policy Howard Lilley decreed that if his son was to come into retailing he would certainly not start his career in the store at Cambridge, and teenager Eaden Lilley found himself learning the ropes at Bentalls at Kingston, all thoughts of farming dismissed from his mind.

Memories
Blue serge to grey flannel

Few, if any, of the representatives and customers dealing with the buyer-manager of Eaden Lilley's menswear department in the 1960s, knew that only a few years earlier he had been pilot to some of the greatest military names in modern history.

The natural reticence of Jack Cox would certainly not allow him to bring it into the conversation, and as far as he was concerned, it was something that happened during his war service and was in the past.

But famous men like Field Marshal Auchinleck and General Orde Wingate of Chindits fame, had particular reasons to be grateful for the quiet expertise of Flying Officer Cox who served with the RAF's Communications Squadron in Delhi, flying a variety of transport and light aircraft. His log-book, a vital reminder for any pilot, contains a variety of important names and details the flights he made around the continent.

Born in 1917 Jack Cox had gone from school into a menswear shop - Foster and Scott in Letchworth, Hertfordshire - where he learned his trade. He later moved to Essex and then Norfolk before the outbreak of war when he joined the Royal Norfolk Regiment, and two years later volunteered for aircrew with the RAF, doing his basic training on Tiger Moths in South Africa before progressing to Blenheim and Baltimore aircraft.

After the war he tried another trade but switched back to menswear in a shop at Rugby, where one of his tasks was to order cap material for the famous school, from Eaden Lilley.

An advertisement for a buyer for Eaden Lilley's menswear department in 1963 prompted an interview with Kenneth Lilley, and then a job as buyer-manager in that department at £90 a month.

He was buying trousers, shirts, ties, coats, boyswear and other items, and reporting direct to Howard Lilley.

"We were a little down the road from the main store at that time, and the firm seemed quite content to let me get on and organise my own department. I was very impressed with the set up, they seemed happy enough to let me jog along as I thought best," he says.

He was given a target buying figure, and it was up to him to spend the money on the items required.

"They were an absolutely wonderful group of people to work for; they gave an overall figure to aim for, but there was no real pressure to achieve those figures. It was only in the latter years that there was a demand for increased revenue.

"Their only real concern was to make sure that the figure increased year on year, and to be honest that was exactly what happened."

He used to receive a basic commission of 1.25 per cent on the year on year increase.

When he first started he had two staff in the clothing department, one on the boy's department and three on outfitting.

"Looking at it from today's point of view I have to say that it was a steady if somewhat fuddy-duddy department. We were always looking for quality material, but were not too heavily driven by fashion, because the men who came into the store were not that fashion conscious.

"My trade was not outlandish fashion; they were largely middle-aged, middle class. People like shop owners, some office workers and bank managers, were our clients."

Hand made silk shirts were also in demand, but the patterns involved had to be discreet and tasteful.

The demand for made-to-measure suits decreased over the years, largely because specialist firms opened up in the town. The department, however, continued to offer a complete alteration service for off-the-peg suits, jackets and trousers. It was also involved with Moss Bros in the hire of formal occasions suits and menswear.

After his stint during the war Jack Cox never had another opportunity to control an aircraft. He concentrated his efforts and time into running the very successful menswear department, and enjoyed almost every moment of his employment with Eaden Lilley, but asked the question "Did you miss flying?" he nods and says quietly, "Yes, oh yes."

Memories
Linking the generations

The dark-green open topped De Dion Bouton of the early 1900s was the pride of the company, a sophisticated motor car with a single cylinder vertically mounted engine providing a top speed of 33 mph - on the flat.

The brainchild of a marquis and a mechanical engineer, the driving controls were complex, but the engine was considered an absolute marvel, and hundreds of the cars were built and sold from the French factory which at its height employed 2,500 workers.

One found itself the mount for the immaculately dressed Bill Lant, a commercial traveller employed by Eaden Lilley, and a man highly successful at his job. His car swept into the towns and villages of his area carrying samples of the firm's goods from grocery through to drapery.

His version of the vehicle had an added extra, not included in the earlier models; it boasted three forward gears and one reverse gear. That meant it could tackle the toughest hills, albeit in reverse, and it gave the man from the department store a cutting edge over his rivals. His style, panache and pure selling skills together with the quality of his goods, meant that he was welcome wherever he went.

Apart from an apprenticeship in Ely, Bill Lant spent his entire working life at Eaden Lilley.

His daughter Nellie, aged 97 in 1999, said :"All his customers thought the world of him. They didn't know what to buy, and he helped and advised them, so that they were able to offer the best goods from their shops."

Up until the arrival of the De Dion the commercial travellers had made their trips around the countryside by train. Bill Lant was the first to be given a car which was housed in the garage at Glisson Road.

Friday nights at the Lant home in Cambridge would involve all three children helping their father count the takings for the week, the notes and coins being separately piled on the table. The commercial traveller had a speedy way of folding the notes so that they could be easily counted, a habit followed by Nellie throughout her life.

Business was good for Bill Lant, and for the firm, and he was able to afford a comfortable house and boats on the river, together with buying a business for his eldest son Humphrey. There was also no need for daughter Nellie to go to work, something that certainly was not done in 1918. But she was, in her own words, a "bit of a rebel" and her parents decided that a spot of work would calm her down slightly. And so at 16, after a short and mutually unacceptable period in a typing school in Trinity Street, she joined her father at the department store, where she found herself working with buyer Miss Maud Knight, a doyen of the childrens' clothes and ladies underwear departments.

During her time at the company she never saw her wages; it was handed to her father and put into a savings account on her behalf. She was, however, given pocket money

Under the watchful eye of Miss Knight, who lived with her mother in Kimberley Road, Nellie learned her craft; she was taught in the art of measurements, costing, estimating and buying, and a regular perk was to visit London with the buyer to consider the latest on design and fashion.

The immaculately dressed Bill Lant.

"In those days all the warehouses were around St Paul's, and when we arrived from the train at Liverpool Street we were welcomed by a chauffeur driven car, and taken to the wholesale premises," remembers Nellie who was later to become Mrs Bowyer.

The apprentice soon found herself searching out her own children's fashions for her customers back in Cambridge who were anxious for a particular style or fashion. The first rule was always that the article should be of good quality. "We were looking for pretty dresses, pretty coats and, of course, school uniforms," she says.

Although both buyer and apprentice wore black while at work, their quest was for a variety of colours and cloth for their customers.

A keen girl-guide, Nellie was given time off to attend camps, and unusually was allowed holidays to fit in with father; normally the last into the department had the worst pick of the holidays.

Her stubborn streak came to the fore during a small dispute with a customer, who immediately complained to the management. She stuck by her guns during the interview with one of the Lilley brothers, with the result that the customer was asked not to shop again at Eaden Lilley.

Miss Knight was a good teacher, strict but fair, and she ran her department of eight on firm lines. She had a soft side, however, and when Nellie became Mrs Bowyer in 1933 she received a superb collection of glassware from the buyer. Her husband Stanley, who was in insurance, was not keen on his wife working and so Nellie left the company just before the wedding.

Like so many people in Cambridge and surrounding district she retained her links with the store. She held an account there, she bought the children's clothes there and she shopped for presents at Christmas.

When her children grew up they also used the store; one family with generations of involvement with the Eaden Lilley department store - a story repeated many, many times.

Chapter 10

The fateful decision

William Eaden Lilley was bored.

He paced the floors of the Market Street store talking to staff and trying to keep himself busy, but there was no doubt that he did not have enough work to do and was rapidly becoming extremely frustrated with his role in the family firm.

He had previously spent more than three years as a trainee with Bentalls of Kingston, had worked in a variety of departments and acted as a department head in one section; had attended management training courses; had spent four months on a highly complicated project involving property owned and rented by the London store; had moved to a Wolverhampton store where he ran departments, and in February, 1976 moved back to Cambridge, with his wife, to work in the personnel department with Geoffrey Heath.

William Eaden Lilley.

But he had too much time on his hands and appeared to be getting nowhere fast. He recalled his father Howard referring to similar problems when he returned to the store after outside training. After six months Howard had moved again to another company before later rejoining W.Eaden Lilley & Co.

In 1976 his son knew there was every likelihood that he would be moving into the senior ranks of the firm, and he wanted to get on with the job of helping to run the business. The personnel work was interesting but not challenging, and although he helped produce employment programmes for school-leavers, he did not feel that it was enough, bearing in mind his experience. He let Geoffrey Heath know his feelings.

"Nothing much happened at first, and then suddenly I found myself with more projects, more work and more direct involvement in the firm. I carried out all the staff interviews up to buyer level and was actively concerned with staff training and other matters. I felt, at last, that I was contributing something really worthwhile to the store."

His father, uncle and other board members appeared to have decided that the time had come to groom him for greater responsibility.

The same year also saw an incident which exemplified the caring approach of the firm, not just to its staff, but also to its customers. It started when John and Mary Bradshaw of Linton visited the store to buy their four-year-old son Alex a bright red and orange scooter for his birthday. All went well until they decided to wrap the present and checked inside to discover it was the wrong size scooter.

They called the store - which by now was closed - by using the 24 hour funeral service line, and were eventually given the home number of chairman Kenneth Lilley. He set off at high speed for the store, selected the right size scooter and drove it out to the Gog Magog roundabout on the outskirts of the city, where the scooters were exchanged. He said later: "Those of us who have children know how much these things mean to them."

By 1978 - the year Prime Minister James Callaghan tried to impose a five per cent pay ceiling resulting in industrial strife, and the so-called "Winter of Discontent" - Michael Marriott joined the company as merchandise director, later to become managing director following the retirement of both Cyril Mack and Frank Webb.

Geoffrey Heath with plans for The Greenhouse restaurant.

The board at that stage consisted of Kenneth and Howard Lilley, Geoffrey Heath, Michael Marriott and financial director Roger Mallabon, also recently appointed. Eaden Lilley was appointed to the board in 1980, and was now looking after a substantial training programme, which later included "fast-tracking" school-leavers with "A" level qualifications. It meant many new entrants going through the same sort of training that he had received during his years with Bentalls of Kingston. An average of 16 trainees a year were put through the course.

"It worked very well. There were a lot of people who benefitted from the scheme. We knew, of course, that some people would move on, but some stayed, and it was important that we had well trained managers within the store," he says.

At that time the company had more than 500 employees, which included part time workers. Even so there was still a cry that the right services could not be maintained unless there were more staff. Over the years which followed staff numbers were reduced as the firm amalgamated buyerships and took out some of the less profitable areas. By its closure in 1999 total staff levels, including concessions were down to under 300.

In theory the big advantage of a family business is that it should be able to make decisions. Not so in the boardroom at Eaden Lilley, which was still largely under the control of majority shareholder Kenneth Lilley.

"Our big problem was that we would agree a course of action at one board meeting, and when the minutes were presented at the next meeting the chairman would like to revisit the problem. The upshot was that we frequently finished up without making a decision - or we took many board meetings to agree on a course of action."

Following many months of debate and planning by 1981 the whole of the second floor of the store was rebuilt to house the carpets and soft furnishing departments from 23, Market Street, together with a restaurant - The Greenhouse - and a hair and beauty salon.

These latter additions finally brought to fruition some of the aspirations Michael Marriott had had since he first joined the company three years earlier. As we have seen, at that time, the "old fashioned" image of the store was overwhelming. One of the many ways in which a rejuvenation could be brought about was to extend customer services with the introduction of up-to-the-minute facilities, which would increase the traffic of target customers. Having come from a department store group in which all its stores had at least one restaurant, it was inconceivable to the merchandise director that Eaden Lilley should not provide such a facility. There had always been a reluctance to go down this particular path, especially on the part of the chairman "for fear of the unknown." The prospect of entering a field about which nothing was known and the thought of employing catering staff - a notoriously mobile and difficult kind of employee to handle - had been enough to put him off. Oddly enough, this was in spite of the fact that quite sophisticated staff catering had been introduced many years previously. However, in the face of Michael Marriott's insistence, and with the enthusiastic support of fellow director and food expert Geoffrey Heath, "The Greenhouse" finally became a reality. It became the responsibility of Geoffrey Heath, who masterminded the design and successfully saw it through every phase of the planning process. This was a thoroughly comprehensive exercise involving not only the physical design, but the determination of the desired ambience, menu planning and staff recruitment. The ultimate triumph was the recruitment, as the first manager, of Mrs Pat Richards, later to become operations director of the entire business. She was appointed to the board at the same time as Graeme Minto, a local entrepreneur and a scientist of international repute, was appointed as a non-executive director.

In an issue in October, 1981 the Cambridge Evening News carried an advertising supplement on the changes. It quoted one of the directors as saying the board had been "astounded by the response" following the opening of The Greenhouse in July that year.

They knew it would be a successful venture, but to find people waiting on the dot of 9.30am for it to open was more than they had hoped for. Customers have been queuing up every day ever since. They come to meet their friends for coffee, husbands to meet their wives for lunch, and at half term holiday it was full of children enjoying a free back-to-school treat.

The big draw is the good wholesome food for which you queue cafeteria style. Croissants, rolls and granary bread come first then the quiche and flans. There is a range of meat - ham and cold beef - for example, and cold fish - crab and salmon - from which to choose, the salad section is most tempting with bowls of walnuts and finely shredded cabbage, tomatoes, sweetcorn and other colourful combinations.

Houseplants, a tiled mural by Sally Anderson and a green and beige colour scheme all contributed to creating The Greenhouse image.

The development also gave the company the opportunity to install new cloakrooms and lifts. Although many customers were said to lament the loss of the lifts with their "sliding cranking bars and the brass fittings,"it was almost impossible for the company to buy new parts for the old lifts and many had to be especially made. The lift space was taken over by the jewellery and perfumery departments.

The moves meant that all departments were now under one roof in Market Street, although there was a warehouse and a funeral department with its private chapel, the photographic laboratory and the cabinet and bedding workshops in Mill Lane, and the firm's garage and another warehouse in Glisson Road.

The restaurant development and other moves followed some tough talking at board meetings, especially by Michael Marriott who had made it clear as early as the spring of 1980 that steps had to be taken to "ensure the survival of the business."

In a confidential memo to his fellow directors he said: "In the present economic climate with trading conditions as they are it is absolutely fundamental for the continued success of the business that we take urgent action in a number of areas." He urged the board to be completely objective, "painfully critical, forthright in expressing our views and resolute in carrying out the action considered to be necessary."

And he added: "I know that this is a family business and I am proud to have been invited to become associated with it, but it must be conducted more professionally.

"Against a background of bitter experience I see the writing on the wall. I believe it is your earnest wish that this business should not only survive, but continue to flourish. We are unanimous in this. But wishing will not make it happen."

He said that the admirable paternalistic philosophy must not be confused, or allowed to be an excuse for amateurism.

Immediate changes he suggested included more training for senior managers, delegation of more responsibilities to buyers and managers, establishing effective lines of communication, increasing the rate of productivity and better forward planning.

And there were some hard facts that had to be faced by senior management, not least, said Michael Marriott that "we do not need the number of people we presently employ to run the business."

During the following 18 months many of the recommendations were carried out including a reduction in staff numbers, reduction in some part-timers hours, rearrangement of delivery schedules and regular financial reports made available each month.

Modernisation in a variety of areas took place in the early 1980s including providing wages by direct bank transfer, and the use of early computers. In 1984 Roger Mallabon declared himself a total convert to computerisation and added: "Sales forecasting used to be a nightmare before we went over to computers. I don't know how we coped.

"We had accounts people sitting for weeks totting up figures with pencil and paper for 50 departments. Now we feed everything into the computer and it comes up instantly with projections for every department for the next six months.

The time saved is enormous and the machine is far more accurate because it never overlooks anything."

The decision to computerise was taken in 1977, with the result, said Roger Mallabon, that the firm had become more competitive and "costly surplus stock had been reduced to a minimum."

The store's system handled all company accounts, purchase and sale reports, payrolls and personnel records for the 400 staff.

The 1982-83 year threatened to be "the most difficult year we have ever experienced," according to a report to the board by Michael Marriott who urged a slight reduction in staff levels. a careful watch on wages, better performance from buyers, a "careful and urgent study" of space utilisation, and a need to reduce the ratio of "chiefs to indians."

A coffee shop was created in-store in 1983 by extending the first floor across the yard, and, a year later, a new warehouse was built at Mercers Row, to replace the two uneconomical buildings at Mill Lane and Glisson Road. The former furniture repository in Mill Lane was developed under a £2.5m scheme and included shops, a wine bar, a bakery, a restaurant and nine offices.

At the same time a young fashion department was introduced as part of the modernisation programme. Named "Pink" the new venture occupied 1000 square feet on the ground floor with its own entrance in Market Street. Its merchandise range covered fashion and accessories geared for the young market and was advertised as "bridging the gap in teenage fashion." It had its own buyer and responsibility for its overall control was placed with Eaden Lilley.

The firm's membership of Associated Independent Stores (AIS) was highlighted in 1984 when the Cambridge Evening News sent a reporter with buyer Joan Leaf when she visited the season's AIS fashion collections in Birmingham where a proportion of the company's buying was done. Emphasis was placed on the exclusivity of the merchandise, much of which was only available to AIS members, as well as the excellent value it represented as a result of collective buying.

In common with other department stores around the country, and elsewhere in Europe, the company also very successfully operated leased departments or "shop in shops" with some of the major fashion and shoe manufacturers of the time. In this way the suppliers were able to place their entire collection in a designated area of the store for which they would provide both the shopfitting design and the staff. In return they paid a percentage of the sales achieved to the store.

By 1985 an extra 1,500 square feet was added to the ground floor by extending into what had formerly been part of the delivery yard and warehouse space to accommodate fine china and crystal collections by the world famous Wedgwood, Royal Doulton and Aynsley. Warmly received by existing customers they were also of particular interest to visiting tourists, especially those from Japan and the United States.

Two years later a spring and summer guide to the store, entitled "In Style at Eaden Lilley," was proudly proclaiming that the firm had more than 100 departments offering "everything from fashion to food, holidays to hair and beauty, and carpets to kitchens." The "independence" of Eaden Lilley was emphasised, "something of a rarity in department stores nowadays," said the guide which explained: "Having no pre-set guidelines to keep to, Eaden Lilley can tailor itself to suit its customers.....the people in and around Cambridge. That means a wide range of lifestyles and age groups all catered for by our team of friendly, caring staff who really know what they are talking about."

October of that year marked a momentous occasion in the company's history when the first branch store was opened in Saffron Walden, Essex.

There had been those on the board who had been advocating the establishment of branches or "satellite stores" for decades, but the spirit of adventure had been lacking and the store had always remained exclusively a Cambridge operation. Early in the 1980s, however, after much research in the region, a very old fashioned and ailing furniture business had been spotted occupying a prime site in the Market Square at Saffron Walden. Enquiries revealed that there was a significant absence of succession in the family which owned the business, which was merely "freewheeling" without making any real progress. As a result of protracted negotiations over a long period, the tenants of the property were persuaded to relinquish it and a new lease obtained from the owners.

The first branch store was opened in Saffron Walden, Essex.

The property, which comprised one half of a handsome building occupying one whole side of the Market Square was transformed into a modern high class fashion store on ground and first floors with a "Rooftops Restaurant" on the second floor.

A few years later, after courting Ridgeons, the owners of the other half of the building for some time, a lease was obtained which enabled the store to be almost doubled in size and now occupied the whole building.

The following year the size of the arcade in the Cambridge premises was reduced to provide more selling space, and automatic doors installed.

In August of the same year, a small neighbourhood store located at Great Shelford, some five miles from Cambridge city centre, was acquired from the owner Ray Douglas, a fellow member of AIS, who was sadly terminally ill and wanted to see the business he had built up "go to a good home." Over the years the shop had earned itself a high reputation under the name Douglas of Shelford and it was decided to continue to operate it under that name.

The country's economic fortunes were bringing problems to retailers and industry alike. In January, 1988 Mrs Thatcher became the longest continuously serving prime minister in the 20th century, but the promise of financial security was crashing around the ears of the Conservative government. The previous October had produced "Black Monday" which wiped some £50m off share values, and mid year figures showing a trade deficit of £1.2billion did little to provide stability, and by the autumn of 1989 interest rates had risen to 15 per cent.

In Cambridge, shops and stores not only had to cope with the roller-coaster of money markets, but an acute shortage of car parking in the city. In a detailed report to the city and county councils, the Chamber of Commerce and others, Eaden Lilley made it clear as early as 1986 that it was not at all enthusiastic about ideas like "park and ride" in isolation. "It is our considered opinion that the only sensible, logical, long term solution to our problem in Cambridge lies in the provisions of substantial underground car parking," said the report.

The small neighbourhood store of Ray Douglas.

The report emphasised the importance of retailing for the city and country as a whole. Sales accounted for more than a quarter of Gross Domestic Product, and retailing had "emerged as one of the most important sectors of the economy as an earner of foreign currency and an investor." More than 10 per cent of the workforce is employed in retailing, and unlike other sectors of industry, retailing has not asked for handouts, "but merely the creation of a climate in which enterprise can flourish.

"For this to happen it is equally necessary to create public confidence in the improvement of shopping areas by drawing up - and implementing - practical schemes for pedestrianisation, adequate car parking and public transport facilities as well as park and ride schemes.

"The shopper expects to be able to shop in comfort with convenient and reliable public transport facilities and adequate car parking close to shops."

The underground parking Eaden Lilley wanted to see was at Parkers Piece where the scheme was "entirely feasible and practical." The report said that for the idea to work it required a dedication to the long term solution, enthusiasm - and money. The store offered to make a contribution of £1 per square foot of occupied space if other retailers followed suit; that would have been a payment of £75,000.

One way or another these were proving to be difficult times for the department store and its management, which were not improved by a street survey which showed that most people saw the store as "fuddy-duddy", the "place for their granny to buy her frocks" according to a local newspaper.

Against a background of recession, in common with other retail operators, the board was also becoming more and more concerned with two immediate needs - one to cut costs and the other to raise more money. Staff reductions were obvious and immediate potential areas for cost savings, and there were some changes in the late 1980s, certain areas of buying were merged and redundancy packages, or early retirement deals offered to some employees. Some left, to be re-employed, on a different basis. Although some long-term employees were unhappy with what was taking place, there is little doubt that there should have been an even bigger reduction in staffing levels at this time.

The major shareholders of the business were Kenneth and Howard Lilley and their two sisters Rachel and Bertha, all of whom were advancing in years. Quite properly they had taken steps to ensure that their children's financial interests in the firm would be protected after they had gone. The inevitable result of this was that the intended beneficiaries of trusts inherited in advance of the demise of their parents, a practical interest in the financial performance of the business as compared with alternative forms of investment.

During the latter half of the 1980s it became clear that pressure was building up for more serious consideration to be given to some of the many acquisition attempts and take-over bids with which the firm was being constantly confronted. In the past those who were actively engaged in the firm had never been in any doubt about how these approaches should be dealt with. They did not want to dispose of the business and there the matter ended. Now it was different. The same emotional attachments were no longer present in the minds of some of the interested parties, some of whom lived abroad and only one of whom played any part in the running of the business. The statutory duty of the directors of the company to act in the interests of the shareholders was also an important issue which could not be swept under the carpet.

In those years, when trading was not easy, an enormous amount of time, energy and money was expended on exploring a variety of options, which, in theory, were open for consideration. These extended from selling part of the building or selling the whole site and transferring the business elsewhere, to developing a shopping centre on the site, of which the store would be a part. In the event none of these schemes was proceeded with, the property inflation bubble burst, and an element of "settling down and getting on with the shopkeeping" was restored.

Matters in the UK and abroad were not improving in 1990; Iraq invaded Kuwait, an international oil embargo was set in place, and the Conservative government set about tearing itself apart with party leader challenges and eventual ballots which resulted in the departure of Mrs Thatcher and the arrival of John Major as Prime Minister.

When Operation Desert Storm swept into action in the first two months of 1991, the board at Eaden Lilley was grappling with a bold and exciting way around its problems - the sale of more than a third of the store to W.H.Smith and a £2.5m refurbishment of the remainder to bring a "touch of the 21st century to Cambridge."

It was to become the biggest, and most complicated, change made to the store in its history, and after a long haul to obtain final agreement, the board effectively handed the refurbishment over to Eaden Lilley who set about the task with enthusiasm.

Opening date for the new look store was set for the autumn of 1993, and the work itself was expected to take six months to complete. Every department was to be affected, some closed, some expanded and all modernised. Architects and engineers were also concerned about the risk of the building "twisting" because part had been cut off at the back, and substantial expertise was required to make sure it was safe as well as attractive.

"Every time the engineer arrived, which was far too often as far as I was concerned, it cost us £10,000," says Eaden Lilley.

More than 100 builders and shop fitters worked their way through the spring and summer months of 1993, but even so there were unexpected structural problems which delayed the completion of the store's new facade. In August that year Eaden Lilley was able to announce that four-fifths of the retail space would be back in action by September. The revamp had seen the end of the furniture, kitchenware, DIY, garden furniture, electrical, haberdashery, toys and stationery departments. There was, of course, a price to pay for the changes and 106 job losses took place in July, of which just over 80 were compulsory redundancies,14 were Saturday staff and a large proportion of the remainder were part time workers. It brought the total number of employees down to less than 200.

The refurbishment also saw the end of some of the store's better known accoutrements, including the magnificent grand staircase which was put up for sale. The solid mahogany stairs had been in the store for 60 years, and were originally crafted by newly qualified carpenter William Baker and two colleagues. It took the three men from Kerridge's workshop six weeks to build the staircase. When, in July, 1993, he revisted the staircase before it was taken out, William Baker, then aged 84, said: "It was not a very difficult job because Kerridge's had the best carpenters in the area."

Fashion was the theme for the new-look store, with an avant-garde interior architecture based on a central atrium with natural daylight on all floors. The ground floor boasted mainly cosmetics and perfumery, fashion accessories and menswear with beds, soft furnishings, fashions, shoes, lingerie and the hair and beauty salon on the first floor. The "jewel in the crown" was said to be the "theatre of food" which was claimed to be the most innovative and exciting eating experience in the area. The new food hall had been operating for several months prior to the grand opening in October, 1993.

The investment in time, money and effort was enormous, and a month before the official opening by Betty Boothroyd, Speaker of the House of Commons, Eaden Lilley was urging the city council to organise a strategy "for making the city centre a viable, attractive and accessible area."

In an interview with the Cambridge Evening News he said: "We have made a colossal investment in rebuilding and refitting the new Eaden Lilley. Before committing ourselves we have in fact teetered on whether to stay on this site or not.

"We had to ask ourselves 'Are we right to be investing this money in this building?' We have worked very hard to make sure that the shareholders' investment will give them the kind of return that they want."

He said it was vital that Cambridge had a strategy for the development of the city centre.

A month before the grand opening Kenneth Lilley, who had been ill for some while, died at the Evelyn Hospital in Cambridge, aged 81. He had been a director of the firm for well over 50 years, chairman for 48 years and had been appointed the store's first president shortly before his death.

He had been educated at Southwold and The Leys School in Cambridge, and during the war served with the Army Transport Unit. His interests away from the store included sailing, walking and hockey; he was on the management committee of the Hundred Houses Housing Society; was actively involved with the Society for the Blind, Toc H and the Rotary Club of Cambridge, and was a former director of the Cambridge Building Society. He was a member of the Emmanuel Reformed Church in Trumpington Street,

Despite areas of procrastination during his chairmanship, he had a first class relationship with the staff at the store, and put his concern for family and people above every other aspect of life. Michael Marriott, who took over the post of chairman in August 1993 said: "Kenneth Lilley was a gentleman in every sense of the word. He had great personal charm and integrity, and a consideration for others which knew no bounds."

The ebullient Speaker of the House of Commons, Betty Boothroyd opened the refurbished store in 1993.

At the same time that Michael Marriott was appointed chairman there were other board changes at the store, as Eaden Lilley took over as managing director. Gillian Lilley, elder daughter of Kenneth Lilley, was appointed a non-executive director.

In time for the new opening Pauline Norman was appointed buyer for fashion, lingerie and corsetry; Jill Little buyer for fashion accessories, and Stephen Seymour, buyer for beds, carpets, tabletop and menswear.

The official opening saw crowds of shoppers outside the store on November 1, 1993 to hear Betty Boothroyd say: "This is the re-birth of Eaden Lilley - it is a fresh new chapter in the history of this very famous business."

The new restaurant and bar, which included a number of different eating areas, was particularly popular in the store, which now had a total staff of 180.

Initial customer reaction to the refurbishment was mixed. Some were delighted with the modern look, others made it clear that they did not like, nor expect the changes.

"It took a long while for the people of Cambridge to realise that it was still Eaden Lilley, and that it retained its ethos. But little by little that worry was worn down, and gradually the customers came back," says Eaden Lilley. One of the changes that had an equal number of critics and supporters, was the introduction of 15 separate concessions within the store, although this was nothing new. The introduction of the first concessions had taken place as long ago as the late 1960s and had developed over the years. Of the 180 staff at the store in 1993, 80 were working in concessions, and were paid by them rather than Eaden Lilley. Many were ex-Eaden Lilley employees. The system worked well and an excellent rapport existed between the company and the concessionaires.

The new look store in 1993.

Two years after the refurbishment had started to lift profits at the Cambridge store, a new look was provided for the Eaden Lilley store in Market Place, Saffron Walden.. The existing fashion departments were realigned, offering a wider range of items, and were joined by a cookshop, haberdashery, linens, gifts and greeting cards departments. Director of operations Pat Richards, who had been with Eaden Lilley for six years, said there had been a perception locally that it was an expensive store, which was not the case. She said the main ethos behind the changes was to create a department store which would serve the local community by introducing an increased range of products.

"If we feel that in the future there is a demand for other products then we will endeavour to satisfy the need. The investment we are making really reflects the confidence we have in Saffron Walden as being a good trading centre. Hopefully by introducing the new departments it will encourage local people to use the town centre."

Rapid changes, which were to be of immense importance to the family owned business, were taking place in the mid 1990s. Over a period of five years the family had lost a whole generation; Kenneth Lilley and his brother Howard, who died in 1994, and both their sisters.

The inevitable result was as had been anticipated. New family shareholders, none of whom worked in the business (apart from Eaden Lilley), and, according to the managing director, "few of whom could claim to appreciate fully what the staff and the people of Cambridge felt about the business."

The events which were finally to lead to the sale of the Cambridge store, really started in 1998 when two offers were made for the Cambridge property. The offers closely followed a set of figures which showed a "significant drop" in the levels of profit predicted, and expected, for the previous year.

The board decided that the offers should at least be made known to the shareholders for them to decide what action should be taken. A meeting with shareholders was held to assess their views, and the two companies were asked to firm-up their offer figures in time for the meeting.

The figures arrived on a Friday prior to the Saturday shareholders meeting. "I think at that point I realised what was going to happen," says Eaden Lilley. 'The figures were so large that I knew that many shareholders would want to accept the proposals."

The shareholders made it clear they wished to pursue the offers. The talks were protracted and produced a series of "false dawns" with a deal expected to be signed in October, then November, then the end of the year and on into the early part of 1999. The proposed deal was by then between the store and a joint venture company, Frame Investments and Portfolio Holdings, who wanted the site for US book chain Borders.

While the talks progressed the managing director and his team had to continue to run the store at Cambridge and those at Saffron Walden and Shelford as though nothing was happening.

When the final offer was made an extraordinary meeting of shareholders was called and the voting, mainly by proxy, resulted in the proposal to accept the offer being carried by a majority with only one shareholder casting a vote against the motion.

The deal was agreed with Frame Investments on Tuesday March 23, 1999 and signed the next day. The staff were told on Thursday March 26. For them it came as a complete shock, many burst into tears, others could simply not believe that it was happening. Among those most distressed by the decision was their managing director.

Chairman Michael Marriott told the staff at the emotional meeting in the store: "This is a very painful moment for us all. Many people here today have invested a great deal in this business - some of you a very large part, if not the whole, of your working lives. That kind of effort and dedication cannot be dismissed lightly. What is happening represents a major tragedy for some and an unexpected and traumatic experience for everyone.

"The Eaden Lilley name has been well known and well respected in retailing for 250 years."

He offered every facilty and every kind of help and advice that could be mustered to help with the job losses, and he added: "We have agonised about this I can tell you. Negotiations have been going on for some time of course, but you will understand how important it is in these matters to maintain confidentiality.

"We are devastated - Eaden Lilley and Mrs Richards who have put so much into planning the future and generating your enthusiasm and loyalty are heartbroken."

The agent acting on the company's behalf told the local press: "Eaden Lilley is the latest of a long line of independent freehold retailers who have been continuously courted by national retailers, developers and investors alike.

"While the department store has recently performed reasonably well, the level of financial proposals from interested parties provided the shareholders with difficult decisions."

Nearly 100 staff members pose for the farewell photograph.

It meant another book store for Cambridge, and Jenny Chapman, business editor of the Cambridge Evening News said, on the day after the announcement, that the move would result in fierce competition. "Borders' declared aim is to capture 20 per cent of the UK market and it entered the fray just 18 months ago."

Eaden Lilley's store was closed in June, 1999 with the loss of 125 jobs. Borders was due to open its store in the late summer of 2000.

A special and poignant issue of the house magazine" W.E.L - fare" was produced in the month of closure. Its cover photograph showed nearly 100 members of staff posing for a farewell photograph. Inside it carried a series of letters from amazed and shocked customers, many of whom referred to the "sad loss" of the store and one in particular which was highlighted in the magazine.

It said: "It is with the deepest regret and sadness that I write to you. I have been a customer since about 1946. It has been a pleasure to shop and to experience a feeling of almost 'friendship' with so many of your assistants. Talking to so many people I realise I am not alone in my feelings of deep regret.

"Cambridge will not be the same without your store."

Managing director Eaden Lilley took over the running of the Saffron Walden store which bears his name, and at the end of 1999 was considering whether the Shelford store should also carry the name. The firm has also acquired a property in Sussex Street, Cambridge for a food hall which was opened to customer enthusiasm in the autumn of 1999. It also retains its photography business in Green Street.

But, whatever happens, the days of the great department store founded in 1750, have gone, and almost certainly, cannot be replaced. For staff, former staff, customers and thousands who knew and loved the Market Street premises, the decision to sell was a mighty blow, and not the wish of many, especially William Eaden Lilley, managing director.